CONCERNING THE TRUE CARE OF
SOULS

Martin Bucer (1491–1551),
from Beza's *Icones*.

*Remember the readings and preachings of
God's prophet and true preacher, Martin Bucer.*

John Bradford, 1555
'Farewell to the University and Town of Cambridge'
The Writings of John Bradford, 1:445

CONCERNING THE TRUE CARE OF
SOULS

Martin Bucer

Translated into English by
PETER BEALE

With an Historical Introduction by
DAVID F. WRIGHT

THE BANNER OF TRUTH TRUST

THE BANNER OF TRUTH TRUST
3 Murrayfield Road, Edinburgh EH12 6EL, UK
P.O. Box 621, Carlisle, PA 17013, USA

*

© Peter Beale 2009
First published 2009
Reprinted 2013

*

ISBN: 978 0 85151 984 5

*

Typeset in 11/15 Adobe Caslon Pro at
The Banner of Truth Trust, Edinburgh

Printed in the U.S.A. by
Versa Press, Inc.,
East Peoria, IL

IN MEMORY

OF

DAVID F. WRIGHT
(1937–2008)

Professor of Patristic and Reformation Studies
in the University of Edinburgh

A DEAR CHRISTIAN FRIEND
WHO INTRODUCED ME TO
MARTIN BUCER

Translator's Preface

Von der waren Seelsorge ('*Concerning the true care of souls*') first appeared in German in Strasbourg, the main centre of Martin Bucer's ministry, in 1538. It was later translated into Czech, and the universal scholarly language of Latin (some years after Bucer's death in Cambridge in 1551), but as far as can be ascertained has never until now been translated into English.

Bucer's style of writing is characterized by long and involved sentences, and the English version which follows is similarly unwieldy; however, it seemed preferable to seek accuracy of translation at the expense of felicity of expression. For the same reason I have retained the somewhat awkward term 'carer of souls' to translate '*Seelsorger*' rather than the more common rendering of 'pastor', and reserved 'pastor' and its derivatives for words directly involving the 'shepherding' concept.

Scripture quotations and allusions have been rendered in the New International Version, except where Bucer's version clearly differs from this. Thus the NIV in Ezekiel 34:16, the verse which is central to Bucer's thesis, reads ' . . . the sleek and the strong I will destroy', while Bucer's rendering (and exposition based on it) requires 'the sleek and the strong I will watch over'.

The German text translated is that provided by Robert Stupperich in volume 7 of *Martin Bucers Deutsche Schriften* (1964).

The small figures in italic (e.g. [90]) refer to the page numbers of that volume, and those not in italic (e.g. [A1a]) are those inserted by Stupperich to indicate the pages of the original printing in 1538. Full-size references in square brackets are additions to Bucer's text (in particular the verse numbers of biblical references), while those in italic indicate corrections to errors made by Bucer.

The bulk of this translation was undertaken at the request and with the encouragement of the late Professor David F. Wright of New College, Edinburgh, during a sabbatical term at Westminster College, Cambridge, in the spring of 1993. I am grateful for the hospitality and encouragement of staff and members of that college. For the mistakes, of which there are doubtless many, I blame no-one but myself.

PETER BEALE
Bulkington
Warwickshire
August 2008

Historical Introduction

David F. Wright

Martin Bucer's stock has been rising steadily since the last decades of the twentieth century. From being a figure 'unknown and misknown',[1] he is increasingly being appreciated as one of the most significant *Reformers in the Wings*.[2] A major cause of his emergence from obscurity is the new critical edition of his works, in three series—German works, Latin works and correspondence—which has been in process of publication, not without some fits and starts, since 1955.[3] In addition to Strasbourg, the Munster research institute of the Heidelberg Academy is the most productive factory of this scholarly enterprise. We look forward in particular to the massive commentaries on the Psalms and Paul's letter to the Romans. In content, if not in accessibility to the reader, John Calvin judged Bucer's commentaries second to none.

Martin Bucer (the German form is Butzer) was born in 1491, the son of a cooper, in Schlettstadt (Sélestat) in Alsace. There he received an influential exposure to the new humanist learning, first in Sélestat's famous Latin school (whose rich library is one of the treasures to be discovered by visitors to Alsace) and then, from 1506-7, in the Dominicans' house. Early in 1512 he was sent on to their convent in Heidelberg, which he finally left in the first months of 1521. Soon he obtained a papal dispensation from his monastic vows, and in the summer of 1522 he married Elisabeth Silbereisen, a former nun from Löwenfeld. If Frau Elisabeth Bucer barely rates a mention in most studies of her husband, that only goes to show, according to biographer Hastings Eells, how shrewd a judge of good women he was.

> Elizabeth Bucer was no scholar, no intellectual genius like her husband, but as a mother and a housekeeper she was worth more than a whole kettle full of rubies . . . Never conspicuous, never a brilliant conversationalist, she possessed none the less a genius for orderliness and economy that provided the stage upon which her husband played the role of hospitable host. If he wrote ponderous treatises, it was because she relieved him of the task of telling bedtime stories. If he took a leading part in colloquies here, there, and every where, it was because his departure made no difference in the perfect functioning of his home. If he showed an energy that was inexhaustible, it was because Frau Elizabeth took upon herself all the enervating worries about the wherewithal of existence. She provided the home and she honored her husband. Honored him by a pious, industrious life that was a model of what a pastor's wife should be.[4]

She stayed at her post during the plague of 1541, which carried her off together with, in a few months, no fewer than five of her children and three other members of the Bucers' Strasbourg household. Even in her dying she had a care for husband Martin's needs. Next spring, as she had urged, he married Wibrandis, the widow of Bucer's close reforming colleague, Wolfgang Capito, who died a fortnight before Elisabeth of the same affliction. Wibrandis was by now something of an expert in marrying leading Protestants. Bucer was her fourth husband, and she outlived him by more than a decade.

But we have run ahead of Bucer's career. During his years as a Dominican he not only became well versed in the order's favourite theologian, Thomas Aquinas, but also developed into a keen Erasmian. He was well prepared to be deeply impressed by Luther at the disputation of Heidelberg in 1518 at which the Wittenberg reformer expounded his distinctive theology of the cross. Soon Bucer was describing himself as a 'Martinian' also. He found Luther's Galatians commentary 'a treasury full of the dogmas of pure theology'. His lifelong commitment to the new evangelicalism was soon sealed, and his independence of his Dominican profession was evident many months before he quit the cloister.

There ensued for Bucer two years of uncertainty—encompassing travel, sometimes in flight, short periods of employment and protection (chaplain to Count Frederick of the Palatinate, pastor at Landstuhl in the service of Franz von Sickingen, preacher at Wissembourg), meetings with humanists, printers and Reformers, including Luther, and attendance at the Diet of Worms in 1521—before he was chased out of Wissembourg's pulpit in May 1523 and pitched up in Strasbourg, where his father had citizen rights. He had found the sphere of his life's work.[5] Within a month the city council permitted him to conduct Bible expositions in Latin (not in German), two months later he was preaching in St Thomas' Cathedral, by August 1524 he was fully installed as pastor of the parish of St Aurelia (the council having definitively usurped the rights of the Cathedral canons and the bishop), and before long he was acknowledged as the *de facto* leader of the reform movement in Strasbourg. There he remained until the spring of 1549, when the political and military reverses inflicted on the forces of German Protestantism issued in the imposition of the Augsburg Interim and made it politic for the city authorities to depose Bucer from his pastoral office.

Among a handful of invitations Bucer chose England, where reform was in full spate under King Edward VI and Archbishop

Thomas Cranmer. After a short period as Cranmer's house-guest he was appointed Regius Professor of Divinity at Cambridge, where he died at the end of February 1551. These last two years were by no means his happiest, nor his most successful. Yet he wrote an ambitious, even visionary, charter for a Christian England entitled *The Kingdom of Christ*, his critique of the first *Book of Common Prayer* (1549) contributed somewhat to the second (1552), he lectured on Ephesians, left a not insignificant mark on some future leaders of the English church, disputed on justification and other hot topics, agitated incessantly for a reformed and revitalized ministry, and found time to be concerned for the poor of the town.[6]

Bucer's quarter-century at Strasbourg will no doubt one day fill a substantial two- or three-volume biography. The most recent comprehensive treatment is Martin Greschat's 1990 life; English readers must make do with the fuller but inevitably dated account of Hastings Eells (1931).[7] Bucer is best known for his attempts at mediating in the 'Supper-strife' between the Lutherans and the Zwinglian Swiss. He witnessed first-hand the failure of the Marburg Colloquy (1529), and when unable to subscribe next year to the *Augsburg Confession*, compiled in the *Tetrapolitan Confession* a third, median way on behalf of South Germany's Protestants. His own understanding of the eucharist passed through several phases, from his initial Lutheranism to a partisan advocacy of the Swiss position until he read Luther's 1528 *Confession* and was persuaded that the dispute was more a *logomachia*, a battle about words, than a disagreement in substance. His efforts for reconciliation achieved some genuine success in the Wittenberg Concord (1536), in co-operation with Melanchthon's kindred spirit. But further progress eluded Bucer, partly because his ingenious resourcefulness made him suspect of unprincipled pliability. Others such as Calvin and Bullinger would grasp this undying nettle.

The Reformed Church of Strasbourg and its pastors, with Bucer chief among them, moulded Calvin's thought and practice in several significant directions during his exile in the city 1538-41. As a result it may be fairer to describe Calvin as Buceran, than to determine, anachronistically, whether, and to what extent, Bucer was a Calvinist. Certainly, through the far-flung influence of the Genevan Reformation, Buceran patterns of evangelical practice and teaching were adopted in all the strongholds of Reformed Protestantism.

From an intra-Protestant ecumenical role Bucer went on, again in close league with Melanchthon, to attempt the impossible—for so it eventually proved—in the form of rapprochement with similarly irenicist Catholics in Germany. In a series of colloquies during 1539-41, reaching a climax at Regensburg (Ratisbon), agreed statements were arrived at on the fall, free will and sin and then, remarkably enough, on justification itself. But no further progress was made, and both Luther and the pope vetoed what had been already drafted.

Reformation Strasbourg seemed an attractive haven, especially in the 1520s and early 1530s, to many of the kaleidoscopic spectrum of radical reformers who were united by few things beyond a conviction that mainstream reform, whether Lutheran, Zwinglian or whatever, had not gone far enough. Bucer was not impervious to their complaints, and his own developing thought, especially on discipline and confirmation, reflected a positive response to them. But the radicals' separatism threatened the continuity of reform in the city, as well as endangering its image in the eyes of outsiders. Bucer spearheaded, through the critical synods of 1533-4, the formalization of the doctrine and order of the reformed church, in tortuous negotiations with the civil authorities which would never concede to the pastors the freedom of movement they believed essential to the creation of an authentic Christian community in Strasbourg. These measures inevitably entailed severer restrictions and sanctions against dissenters. They also accompanied, and reflected, a steady evolution in Bucer's mind that took him nearer to Luther and placed greater confidence in the external forms of sacraments and ordinances.

Beyond Strasbourg, Bucer was in demand for the drawing up of reformed church orders, in locations as diverse as Ulm, the territory of Hesse and the archdiocese of Cologne. The Hessian ordinance perhaps comes nearest to embodying, in the greatest detail, Bucer's ideals of Christian discipline, although its main lines are substantially the same as those of the earlier Strasbourg ordinance. The Ziegenhain synod, whose outcome was this disciplinary order for Hesse, was held in November 1538, the year in which Bucer published the treatise on True Pastoral Care translated in this volume. Some of the ideas spelt out in this treatise were transcribed into the forms of the Ziegenhain ordinance.[8]

This is, then, an appropriate moment at which to turn from this broad-brush summary of Bucer's reforming ministry (though nothing has been said, for example, of his inspiration of Strasbourg's reshaped and innovative educational system, or of his contributions to liturgical and ministerial renewal which, in a Genevan form, influenced Reformed practice), and to focus in on the work before us. Its full title in German is *Von der waren Seelsorge und dem rechten Hirten dienst, wie derselbige inn der Kirchen Christi bestellet, uund verrichtet werden solle.* (The sub-title is considerably longer!)[9] It translates fairly literally as *Concerning the true soul-care and the correct shepherd-service, how the same should be established and executed in the church of Christ.*

The work issued from the press of the Strasbourg printer, Wendel Rihel, probably in April 1538,[10] as seems indicated by a letter from Bucer to Ambrosius Blaurer, soon to move from Württemberg to Augsburg, of April 4, 1538, in which he explained why he felt compelled to write the work:

Both appreciation and concern for the community of the saints [*cura communionis sanctorum*] are extinguished more every day, and even pastors themselves seem to be ever less aware of what pastoral care [*cura pastoralis*] is. I reckoned that I must counter this calamitous situation, and I have published something on it [*ea,* i.e. *cura pastoralis*], which I am sending you.[11]

When representatives of the Bohemian Brethren visited Strasbourg in 1540, they bore a letter to Bucer from their bishop, Jan Augusta, which expressed a particular interest in having *Von der waren Seelsorge* translated into Czech.[12] In reply, Bucer expressed his pleasure at their appreciation of it, and explained that he had written it for the benefit of those who sought in the ministry of the Strasbourg pastors more a way of casting off the papal yoke than of submitting to the yoke of Christ. They detested discipline beyond reason.[13]

Bucer told Augusta of his dissatisfaction that he had not treated so critical a subject in the manner it merited. But since so few tackled it, he had done his best, at least in enunciating certain guidelines. The work bears evidence of having been compiled in some haste, but then Bucer was never a polished wordsmith, and its forcefulness and clarity carry the day. That he continued to regard it highly is attested by his mentioning it among his half-dozen or so major writings in his last will and testament drawn up in 1548. *Von der waren Seelsorge* embodied the teaching on church ministry, discipline and the communion between Christ and his members in which he prayed God ever to keep himself and his family.[14]

Yet by no means all his contemporaries in Strasbourg welcomed it. Bucer's most recent biographer has commented that hardly any other work by the city's leading and by now famous theologian was so emphatically ignored by ruling circles in Strasbourg.[15] The reason for this almost deliberate snub lay in the book's challenge to the magistrates (i.e. the city council) at a particularly sensitive point—the control of church discipline. Bucer and his colleagues had been pressing on this door for some years, but so far with quite limited success. For Bucer, more lucidly than any Reformer to date, was firmly of the conviction that discipline belonged with the word and the sacraments as constitutive marks of the church of Christ. All three were the essential responsibility of the church's ministry, so that the task of ministry could be characterized in terms of these three functions. The triad became increasingly prominent in Bucer's writings from the later 1530s.[16]

It is true that one does not find this threefold division explicitly enumerated in *True Pastoral Care*—which may have something to do with what its modern editor, Robert Stupperich, calls its *'Augenblickscharakter'*,[17] the impression of precipitate immediacy that its text conveys. But the prominence of discipline will escape no reader. 'There are two sorts of ministry . . . the ministry of the word and discipline, and the ministry of temporal care for those in need' (p. 29). The former can just as easily be called 'The ministry of teaching and spiritual discipline' (p. 26) or 'the ministry of the care of souls' (p. 30). And when Bucer lists 'the five main tasks of the care of souls', a disciplinary ethos breathes through them all.

> First: to lead to Christ our Lord and into his communion those who are still estranged from him, whether through carnal excess or false worship. Secondly: to restore those who had once been brought to Christ and into his church but have been drawn away again through the affairs of the flesh or false doctrine. Thirdly: to assist in the true reformation of those who while remaining in the church of Christ have grievously fallen and sinned. Fourthly: to re-establish in true Christian strength and health those who, while persevering in the fellowship of Christ and not doing anything particularly or grossly wrong, have become somewhat feeble

and sick in the Christian life. Fifthly: to protect from all offence and falling away and continually encourage in all good things those who stay with the flock and in Christ's sheep-pen without grievously sinning or becoming weak and sick in their Christian walk (p. 70).[18]

At the same time, this summary reveals only too well that, for Bucer, discipline was considerably broader than the preoccupation with inquisitorial, punitive and exclusive processes in connection with a narrow category of serious offences that 'discipline' has come to connote, especially in areas of Reformed Christianity. A recent excellent study by Professor Amy Nelson Burnett of the University of Nebraska-Lincoln distinguishes between 'church discipline', i.e, measures administered by the church specifically for the correction of sinners, and 'Christian discipline'. She cites a definition of 'the discipline of Christ' that Bucer included in one of his earliest letters from England to the pastors of Strasbourg. It consisted in this,

> that all the members of Christ recognize and embrace each other most intimately and lovingly, and that they build one another up in the knowledge of and obedience to the Son of God most zealously and efficaciously, and that the ministers of the churches know, care for and tend the individual sheep of Christ, as the chief pastor Christ set the example.... In countless places in Scripture, the Lord described and set forth for us this [discipline] which we also have proclaimed so clearly for so many years in life and writings and sermons.[19]

The responsibility of fellow Christians to care for and admonish each other is not to the fore in *True Pastoral Care*, which chiefly attends to the responsibilities of pastors. Nevertheless, the first section defines the church as the membership of all Christians one of another, 'each having his office and work for the general good of the whole body and all its members' (p. 1). 'Christians are to look after one another most faithfully not only in spiritual but also in temporal matters' (p. 6).[20] What emerges at the outset in these few simple but moving pages is of cardinal significance for the whole treatise.

Although Bucer's ministry was set in a state-church context (the state being the city, and the church in theory co-terminous with it, with virtually the whole population baptized), his goal was never less than the building up of a community of true Christians, who have 'really come to know Christ our Lord' (p. xxvii), 'really faithful Christians, who have genuinely trusted in Christ and given themselves over to a heartfelt obedience to the gospel' (p. xxxiii). Bucer's ecclesiology always lived in some degree of tension between these two poles, as is demonstrated masterfully in the title of Gottfried Hammann's essential work (in French) *Between the Sect and the City*—on Bucer's church-programme or blueprint (*projet d' Eglise*).[21] The two poles can be variously characterized—majority church, people's church (cf. German Volkskirche), the Augustinian *corpus permixtum* on the one hand, and on the other the confessing church, community of believers, *communio sanctorum*. Riding both horses could be very uncomfortable. Bucer's continued insistence on the universality of infant baptism (against Strasbourg's numerous Anabaptists) was accompanied by its inevitable depreciation in favour of a quasi-sacramental confirmation (on which Burnett's book is particularly helpful).[22]

True Pastoral Care's heavy attention to Christian discipline is explicable in this frame of reference, for Christian discipline is what will transform the church of the masses—the people who think 'that if they have been baptized and take part in the common ceremonies, and do not interfere in the affairs of the so-called priests, that they belong to the church and congregation of Christ' (p. xxvii)—into a fellowship of true Christians, or at least will fashion the latter within the bosom of the former. In this way, the Strasbourg pastors could turn the edge of the radicals' criticisms.

> This little book will also show all pious Christians how the leaders of the sects falsely accuse us of teaching a faith which is devoid of fruits and works, and not insisting that our people embrace the true fellowship and distinguishing marks of the body of Christ and Christian discipline (p. xxxII).

Hence the necessity of the introduction of a system of evangelical penance, on which this treatise expatiates at such length.

Bucer was well aware of the dangers of penance—first, that some would be driven completely away from the church; second, that others would 'play the hypocrite by an outward show of penance'; and third, that yet others would be plunged in despair (p. 128)—but they served to reinforce the diligence and earnestness to be applied to the provision of really suitable pastors and elders. Another objection gave him the opportunity to put beyond doubt that penance did not bestow forgiveness of sins, which were pardoned only by the mercy of God through the blood of Christ (and Bucer remained very nervous of private absolution), but was directed to sharpening recognition of present and aversion to future sins (p. 129).

One salient element in Bucer's argument is the appeal to the teaching and example of the early church. Such increasing reliance on patristic authority is a marked feature of Bucer's theology from the mid-1530s. But it laid him open to an accusation of anachronism.

> They . . . say: in our churches, where now everyone is baptized and is supposed to be a Christian, there is not the opportunity to practise discipline and penance that there was in the churches of the apostles and martyrs, when the congregations were small in number and those who wanted to be Christians were driven close

together by persecution and were kept in humility and serenity. This is because no-one would profess the faith unless he was serious about it (p. 144).

The charge illustrates the modern resonance of Bucer's work. He counters it easily enough. In the age of the fathers, churches were often more populous than ones in Strasbourg, and yet they maintained this practice of discipline—and they needed to, for there were no fewer wicked goats or sickly sheep among Christ's flock then than there are now (p. 148).

Throughout the treatise Bucer upholds the high responsibility of pastors to abandon none of the baptized (p. 88-9). 'The faithful ministers of Christ must not give up lightly on anyone' (p. 78). Bucer insists with emphatic repetition that the Great Commission is in no degree compromised by the hiddenness of God's election. 'The fact that all people have been made by God and are God's creatures should therefore be reason enough for us to go to them, seeking with the utmost faithfulness to bring them to eternal life' (p. 77). Bucer has some repute as the most missionary-minded of the leading Reformers.

But the objection which probably cut deepest, and frightened off even the God-fearing, contemplated in the reformed soul-carers' assumption of disciplinary powers a recrudescence of the old violence and tyranny of pope and priests (p. 152). Bucer has his response, of course: papal and sacerdotal power mounted on the back not of church discipline and penance but of accumulating wealth and entanglement with princely courts. But it was probably this fear more than any other factor that led to the official silence which *True Pastoral Care* met with in Strasbourg. The clergy had met with a damaging reverse in the crucial Strasbourg synods of 1533, when the magistrates so emended the draft ordinance that the decisive role in the discipline of the laity was left in the hands of representatives of the city council. Bucer was frustrated, but not defeatist. *True Pastoral Care* was his most extended manifesto, in the years following the 1533 synods and the 1534 ordinance, in a continuing campaign to convince the people of Strasbourg of the necessity of independent pastoral competence in the disciplinary realm. The work in no sense debarred magistrates from the promotion and protection of true religion and godly behaviour. But it highlights

> the difference between the discipline and correction of rulers and the discipline and correction of carers of souls. Even when the civil authority exercises its office of warning against and punishing wrong with the greatest diligence, it is still necessary for the church to have its own discipline and correction ... It is not only that this ecclesiastical discipline is more exactly suited to the conscience, but also that it has as well as its own command, its own spiritual success and fruit, through the Spirit of our Lord Jesus Christ. These are the keys to the kingdom of heaven. (p. 144).

There is indeed much more in this 'masterwork of pastoral theology'[23] than the theme of discipline. But it is arguably the most distinctive thread running through it, as Bucer still endeavours to carry forward the citywide church in his pursuit of a church of true believers. Several years later, in the later 1540s, he seemed to despair of adequate backing from the civil authorities and their designated church-wardens (*Kirchenpfleger*), and turned instead to a voluntary system of pledged commitment to the demands of evangelical piety. These 'Christian fellowships' (*Christliche Gemeinschaften*) were essentially rolls of freely enlisted parishioners who submitted themselves to precisely the kind of disciplinary scrutiny that in *True Pastoral Care* Bucer still aspired to have applied to the whole baptized population.[24]

This focus on discipline is justifiable for a further reason: it is probably this dimension of *True Pastoral Care* that at first sight will appear most alien to congregations of the churches of the Reformation in the rapidly de-Christianizing West. Yet by the very same token it may offer the sharpest challenge, and the largest hope, to Christian communities seeking to attain a distinctive identity amid such confusion.

ENDNOTES

[1] To coin a word in translating the title of Jean Erbes, *Martin Bucer, le Réformateur Alsacien Inconnu et Méconnu* (Strasbourg: Librairies Protestantes, 1966). Note also the title of Peter N. Brooks' 1991 quincentenary sermon at Cambridge, 'Martin Bucer: Oecumeniste and Forgotten Reformer', in *Expository Times* 103 (1991-2), pp. 2321-5.

[2] David C. Steinmetz, *Reformers in the Wings* (1971; Baker Book House, 1981), pp. 121-32.

[3] Details to date in D. F. Wright (ed.), *Martin Bucer. Reforming Church and Community* (Cambridge: Cambridge University Press, 1994), pp. xii-xiii.

[4] Hastings Eells, *Martin Bucer* (New Haven: Yale University Press, 1931), pp. 415-6.

[5] It is an oddity of the much-used *Oxford Dictionary of the Christian Church* (ed. F. L. Cross) that for two editions its article on Bucer has not mentioned Strasbourg.

[6] For recent accounts of his English period, with references to other studies, see the late Basil Hall's 'Martin Bucer in England', in Wright (ed.), *Martin Bucer*, pp. 144-60; D. F. Wright, 'Martin Bucer and England—and Scotland', in Christian Krieger and Marc Lienhard (eds), *Martin Bucer and Sixteenth Century Europe. Actes du colloque de Strasbourg* (28-31 août 1991), 2 vols. (Studies in Medieval and Reformation Thought LII; Leiden: E. J. Brill, 1993), II, pp. 523-32; id., 'Martin Bucer (1491-1551) in England', in *Anvil* 9 (1992), pp. 249-59.

[7] Greschat, *Martin Bucer. Ein Reformator und seine Zeit* (Munich: Verlag C. H. Beck, 1990); for Eells see n. 4 above (it was reprinted, New York: Russell & Russell, 1971). In English note also Miriam U. Chrisman, *Strasbourg and the Reform* (New Haven: Yale University Press, 1967); the introduction to D. F. Wright (transl. and ed.), *Common Places of Martin Bucer* (Courtenay Library of Reformation Classics p. 4; Appleford: Sutton Courtenay Press, 1972); W. P. Stephens, *The Holy Spirit in the Theology of Martin Bucer* (Cambridge: Cambridge University Press, 1970); and Amy Nelson Burnett, *The Yoke of Christ: Martin Bucer and Christian Discipline* (*Sixteenth Century Essays and Studies* XXVI; Kirksville, MO: Sixteenth Century Journal Publishers, 1994). This last, despite its specific focus, provides a good overview of the chief phases of Bucer's career. Finally, those charged with ministries of Christian education may wish to know of the cartoon-style A4 size booklet (35 pp.) written by Gottfried Hammann and Englished by R. Gerald Hobbs (both eminent Bucer scholars), *Martin Bucer*, in a series 'Leaders of Protestantism Past and Present', published by Editions du Signe, Eckbolsheim, Strasbourg (ISBN 2-87718-061-1).

[8] See Burnett, *The Yoke of Christ*, pp. 113-21.

[9] See below, p. xxvii.

[10] For publication details, including later editions, see *BDS* 7, pp. 84-9. The work is no. 59 in the standard bibliography, *Bibliographia Bucerana*, by Robert Stupperich (published with and following Heinrich Bornkamm, *Martin Bucers Bedeutung für die europaische Reformationsgeschichte*, as *Schriften des Vereins für Reformationsgeschichte* 169, Gutersloh: C. Bertelsmann Verlag, 1952), at p. 53. A Latin translation was published in the posthumous collection of his 'English Writings', *Scripta Anglicana* (Basel, 1577), pp. 260-356, *De vera animarum cura . . .*, Stupperich, *Bibliographia*, nos. 59a, 115. Internal features make it clear that this was not Bucer's own work, but executed for him while at Cambridge, quite possibly by his secretary-cum-domestic assistant, Martin Brem (see *BDS* 7, pp. 85-7).

[11] T. Schiess (ed.), *Briefwechsel der Brüder Ambrosius Blaurer und Thomas Blaurer, 1509-67*, 3 vols. (Badische Historische Commission; Freiburg-im-Breisgau:Fehsenfeld, 1908-12), I, p. 873 no. 806 (correcting *BDS* 7, p. 69 n.1). Six weeks later Bucer asked Blaurer for his frank opinion of the book; *ibid.* I, p. 877 no. 811, 16 May 1538.

[12] [Amadeo Molnar], 'La correspondance entre les Frères Tchèques et Bucer 1540 à 1542', in *Revue d'histoire et de philosophie religieuses* 31 (1951), 102-56, at 118 (where the date 1541 is a slip; see 105 and n. 4). For the Czech translation, Stupperich, *Bibliographia*, nos. 59f., *BDS* 7, pp. 88-9. It was published in 1543.

[13] Bucer to Augusta, 22 June 1540, in Molnar's French translation, *art. cit.*, pp. 120-21. For the two yokes, Burnett, *The Yoke of Christ*, I, p. 224.

[14] J. W. Baum, *Capito und Butzer Strassburgs Reformatoren* (Elberfeld:

R. L. Friderich, 1860), pp. 569-74, at p. 570. Already in an earlier will, of December 1541, the year of the plague in Strasbourg, Bucer presented this list of his most important works: see *Martin Bucer Strasbourg et l' Europe. Exposition à l'occasion du 500e anniversaire du réformateur stras-bourgeois Martin Bucer 1491-1991* (Strasbourg: Eglise Saint-Thomas, 1991), p. 175 no. 239.

[15] Greschat, *Martin Bucer,* p. 160.

[16] Burnett, *The Yoke of Christ,* p. 98 n. 29, p. 171 n. 34.

[17] *BDS* 7, p. 69.

[18] Summarized at the end as: 'searching for and finding all the lost sheep, bringing back the strays, healing the injured, strengthening the ailing, and guarding the healthy ones and feeding them in the right way' (p. 212).

[19] Burnett, *The Yoke of Christ,* p. 1.

[20] See also, for example: 'the wounded sheep are to be given treatment by all Christians, but particularly by the carers of souls' (p. 53); 'All Christians are to help to bring sinners to repentance' (p. 54).

[21] *Entre la secte et la cité. Le projet d' Eglise du Réformateur Martin Bucer (1491-1551)* (Geneva: Labor et Fides, 1984). Note also his essay, 'Martin Bucer: sa vision de l'Eglise selon le traité "Von der waren Seelsorge" et développement de la discipline ecclésiastique à Strasbourg de 1524 à 1549', in Marc Lienhard (ed.), *Croyants et sceptiques au XVIe siècle. Le dossier des 'Epicuriens' (Societé Savante d' Alsace et des régions de l' Est, Recherches et Documents* 30; Strasbourg: Librairie Istra, 1981), pp. 73-89.

[22] See D. F. Wright, 'Infant Baptism and the Christian community in Bucer', in Wright (ed.), *Martin Bucer,* pp. 95-106.

[23] Burnett, *The Yoke of Christ,* p. 87; see her discussion of *Von der waren Seelsorge, ibid.* pp. 105-13. In Dutch there is a good study by Willem van't Spijker, *De Ambten bij Martin Bucer* (Kampen: J. H. Kok, 1970), pp. 159-77.

[24] Burnett's treatment of these 'fellowships' is an important corrective of earlier studies: *The Yoke of Christ,* pp. 180-207.

Concerning the True Care of Souls and Genuine Pastoral Ministry,

and How the Latter Is to Be Ordered and Carried Out in the Church of Christ

by Martin Bucer.

Here You Will Find the Essential Means whereby
We Can Escape from the Present so Deplorable and
Pernicious State of Religious Schism and Division
and Return to True Unity and Good Christian Order
in the Churches.

Knowledge Which Is Useful
Not Only to the Congregations of Christ,
But also to Pastors and Rulers.

Printed at Strasbourg by
Wendel Rihel,
A.D. 1538.

[91]To all believers in our Lord Jesus Christ, grace and peace from God our heavenly Father and our only Saviour and Head, Jesus Christ, that they may rightly recognize and love his church and the fellowship of his people.

We all acknowledge that we believe in one Christian church, that is, one fellowship of saints, and that we must constitute and have such a church and fellowship, in which the faith which we confess in God, Father, Son and Holy Spirit, is a true and living one. However, the nature of this church and fellowship, what its extent is, what rule and regulation it is to have, is fundamentally so little recognized that it befits anyone who really considers this lack to be filled with pity. Those who still undertake the propagation and defence of the papistical tyranny and abuse accuse us, whom they call Lutherans, of separating ourselves from the Christian [92] church and fellowship, demolishing its order and rule, and destroying the discipline and obedience of believers. But when we turn to the truth we find that on the contrary it is they who have not only torn and disturbed the church of Christ [A2b] and all true fellowship of the saints in Christ, but completely swallowed up and eradicated all understanding of the church and fellowship of believers in Christ.

For the people have been led by them into thinking that if they have been baptized and take part in the common ceremonies, and do not interfere in the affairs of the so-called priests, then they belong to the church and congregation of Christ, even though they may never really have come to know Christ our Lord, and live in

xxxi

open sin, relying for their comfort in God not on Christ, but on the ceremonies of the so-called priests, their own good works, and the merits of dead saints. Indeed, they would be unable to place their trust in Christ the Lord, since in all their life and conduct they contemptuously despise him and his holy word.

From all the popish teaching, who would realize that in Christ we are to have one heart and one soul, and to be his body and members together in him, if in any sense we are to be Christians? And that no-one can be a member of the Lord and of his church and at the same time a member and relative of the world? Where are the innocent servants of Christ who bring Christ's sheep nothing but the Lord's voice and word, [93] who are zealous to seek all the Lord's lost sheep, to bring back those which have gone astray, to heal the injured, to strengthen the weak, to guard the strong and feed them aright [Ezek. 34:16]? And also to shut out from the congregation of Christ all those who [A3a] do not wish to listen to the Lord's word and mend their ways? Yes, who knows less about the whole matter of obedience to the gospel, church discipline, repentance of sins and Christian order; who by life and conduct opposes these to a greater and worse extent, than our pope, with his cardinals, bishops and all their entourage? Yet these are the ones who cry out against us and accuse us of apostatizing from the church and destroying its discipline and rule!

These are the ones we have to thank that so few people know or consider what sort of fellowship the Christian church is, what order and rule it should have, how our only King and Lord Christ rules us in his kingdom and makes us holy. And that is how it is that obedience to the holy gospel and church discipline is still so unknown and despised, even among those who wish to be seen as recognizing the papistical abuse and wanting to flee from it and submit themselves to the yoke of Christ.

Moreover Satan, just as at the beginning of the gospel, at the time of the dear apostles, and whenever the truth of Christ has sought to break out more strongly, and so since the Lord has let the light of his holy gospel illuminate us again, has awakened all manner of sects and heresies; and since each of these heresies claims to be the church, they have torn many naïve hearts away from the true fellowship of Christ, or at least caused manifold hindrances to those who are completely [94] [A3b] committed to the congregation of Christ. This is what this carnal crowd is like, seeking under the name of Christian freedom nothing but carnal impudence and declining above all to put up with Christian correction and discipline, and at the same time not being idle in constantly throwing off the yoke of Christ and doing all in their desire and power to hamper all the order of the church.

It is this tool of antichrist, and certainly not the Lutheran doctrine (which teaches how to trust completely in Christ and also to commit oneself to entire obedience to his word), which has resulted in so few, even of those who do not themselves claim to be the congregation of Christ, rightly understanding or wanting to promote the fellowship, discipline and rule of the church.

We want to demonstrate to all the pious children of God, who from their hearts pray for the future of the kingdom of Christ, according to the measure of our faith, our own duty in this so deplorable scattering of the church, so that they may thoroughly understand what the church of Christ is, what rule and order it must have, who its true ministers are and how they are to exercise their ministry in the care of souls and the pastoral office for the true salvation of Christ's lambs; so that we may at last be a true and rightly ordered church of God and the body of Christ, which we have to be or else be eternally cast out from Christ the Lord and his kingdom.

This is why we have undertaken the writing of this little book concerning all these matters, inserting various quotations from the word of God [A4a] and, insofar as the Lord has given us grace, explaining them. From these every Christian can thoroughly learn what sort of fellowship the church of Christ is, how Christ the Lord alone rules, what ministry he requires in that rule and how this ministry is to be ordered and performed, in relation to all those who are brought to the church of Christ and wish to be kept and built up in it.

We have throughout set out the scriptural quotations, so that the Christian reader can himself see the foundation of the word, consider it [95] and lay it up in his heart. For there are not a few who, as soon as anything is said about church discipline and order, are always crying out that we want to bring back the traditions and bondage of men; and so we do not wish to put forward anything other than the obvious and certain teaching and clear undoubted command of our Lord Jesus Christ.

The unity of the church consists not in having the same ceremonies, but in having the same doctrine, faith, and right administration of the sacraments.

From this it will be seen if we, who are called Lutherans, desire to separate ourselves from the Christian congregation, or are seeking to escape the authority and discipline of the church, and shun the true exercise of repentance with prayer, fasting and everything else. Those who call upon our dear Lord Jesus Christ in truth, whatever their outward customs and identity may be, we wish to acknowledge and love as our members in Christ the Lord. And let them also treat us in the same way, irrespective of the fact that we may not share the same ceremonies and church practices. For the fellowship of the Christian church consists not in ceremonies and outward practices, but in true faith,[A4b] in obedience to the pure gospel, and in the right use of the holy sacraments as the Lord has ordained them. Everything else each church has to arrange as it finds best for itself. In any case this is something which the old holy fathers recognized and maintained.

We have separated from the antichrists, not from anyone in authority over the church.

We do not, therefore, wish to tear ourselves away from any authority in the church. But there is no authority or power in the church except that which is for its good. We gladly listen to the ministers of Christ, whoever they may be and whatever title they bear. But if we are to be Christ's sheep we must run away from those who have a stranger's voice [John 10:5]. Those who bring another gospel we must regard as accursed, even if they were angels from heaven [Gal. 1:8]. As for those who are idolaters, robbers of churches, those whose whole lives are stained by the most hideous vices, but claim to be brothers and members of the church, we must have nothing at all to do with them and reject them completely. This is even more seriously to be observed when these people claim for themselves a greater authority in the church, like the pope, cardinals and bishops. This we are [96] instructed to do not only in holy scripture, but also by all the ancient councils of the church. Were we not to separate from these false and godless church leaders and choose true and faithful ministers, we would lose our fear of God, violate the Lord's command, and stain ourselves with the godlessness of the false ministers. This was recognized and written with great [A5a] solemnity by the holy martyr and bishop Cyprian in his fourth epistle. Indeed, the ancient holy fathers agree with him, both in the decrees of the councils and in their own writings. Therefore no-one is in a position to accuse us in any way of being a sect which has apostatized from the church and its obedience.

Repentance and Christian discipline and practices have been driven out and
destroyed by the papists.

In the same way we do not want to omit anything in restoring
repentance, discipline, and all spiritual practices like prayer, fasting
and the rest, to their proper value and godly use, so that nothing
should hinder us in this any more; because the people have been
reduced by the popish seducers to a state where they know nothing at all about genuine, heartfelt prayer, fasting and penitential
practices, even considering them to be a strange and loathsome
thing. So the poor apostate Vicel and those like him must attribute
this false teaching not to us, but to their popes, bishops and priests,
because we faithfully teach the true and living faith in Christ, to
whom alone is due all true repentance and godly mortification of
the flesh. Therefore we continuously preach the necessity of these
fruits of the Spirit; but their pope, bishops and priests, whom they
claim to be the catholics, are ignorant both of faith in Christ and of
the true fruits of faith, instead contradicting to the greatest degree
both by life and by conduct all faith and repentance—as, sadly, can
all too horribly be seen by all the world.

The sects falsely slander the true doctrine by comparing it with the 'weed' which
in fact they are planting and growing together with their father, Satan.

This little book will also show all pious Christians how the leaders of the sects falsely accuse us of teaching a faith which is devoid
of fruits and works, [A5b] and not insisting that our people embrace
the true fellowship and distinguishing marks of the body of Christ
and Christian discipline. But our doctrine, and our faithfulness
and diligence in proclaiming it, are in no way to be blamed for
the fact that the fruit of faith and Christian [97] discipline is so far
observed only feebly in the mass of people who belong to us. We
read in the gospel and the writings of Paul and all the ancient
holy fathers that really zealous Christians will never constitute a

great number [Matt. 7:13; 20:16; Luke 1:32; Rom. 11:5 &c]. This is what the Lord himself, his holy apostles and the most precious martyrs have preached.

And yet, praise God, there are to be found on all sides many really faithful Christians, who have genuinely trusted in Christ and given themselves over to a heartfelt obedience to the gospel through the doctrine of Christ which he has granted us to maintain. With regard to what is still lacking, this can be put down to the truth that the cause of it lies with Satan, the corrupted nature of our flesh, the devastation wrought by popery, and the way in which the sect leaders and their disciples constantly cast poisonous slander on true doctrine and urge withdrawal from the fellowship of Christ, and by no means with the holy and blessed doctrine of Christ which he has imparted to us. And it is also true that only evil could come from the doctrine of the sects, which is claimed to be in line with the life of the disciples; for, sadly, we daily learn in only too gruesome a way that with their handful of disciples they are offering us desert, thorns and thistles in the place of figs and grapes [Matt. 7:16]. For the true fruit of the Spirit is *love, joy, peace, patience, kindness,* [A6a] *goodness, faithfulness, gentleness and self-control* [Gal. 5:22]. And those belonging to this company are not those who seek the Lord with all their hearts, but those who reject and avoid such, falsely accusing them, believing and propagating all manner of untruths about them, pleasing themselves, being envious, spiteful, selfish, and often, despite all appearance and boasting of possessing a higher spirit, falling into chaotic sexual immorality, as is horribly evident every day amongst the poor eccentrics. However, we will not and ought not judge anyone's doctrine from the lives of those who glory in that doctrine, but only [98] according to the word of the Lord, which alone is infallible.

In this little book we have by his grace held to that same eternal word of the Lord, not just according to the letter (although that, too, is of God), but according to the true spirit and power of the Lord, and set forth the nature, character, law, order and government of the church of Christ from that same word of God alone, not from any human composition. In this way all pious Christian souls are to see that in what follows we are not seeking anything else, other than the true increase of the kingdom of our Lord Jesus and its genuine and authentic fruit. And in doing this it was not our intention even to the slightest degree to hurt or offend anyone anywhere, whatever he does or intends to do, who is in Christ— we emphasize 'in Christ', our dear Lord, to whom everything else must be subordinated. We rather desire gladly to open up and offer in [A6b] the friendliest way the bosom of Christ, so large and wide, only so that he who bought us at so great a price [1 Cor. 7:23] might remain our Lord and Saviour, and we his kingdom and body.

May he grant that at last we may rightly understand that we possess everything good in him alone, and without him eternal death; in this way we will easily deny ourselves all things and devote ourselves entirely to his word and Spirit. In this way also we will become of one heart and soul in him, becoming through his nurture in his kingdom ever freer of the old nature and stronger in his new life; and thus belong to him as living, mature members of a healthy and holy body, to his eternal praise and the increase of his holy kingdom. Amen.

MARTIN BUCER,

*A Minister of the Holy Gospel
in the Church at Strasbourg.*
[1(B1)a]

I

The Fellowship of Christians; The Nature of the Church

The church of Christ is the assembly and fellowship of those who are gathered from the world and united in Christ our Lord through his Spirit and word, to be a body and members of [99] one another, each having his office and work for the general good of the whole body and all its members.

This is to be learnt from the following texts.

Ephesians 4 [:1-6]

Christians deny themselves, have one God, one Christ, one Spirit, baptism and hope, are one body, united to one another in the highest love.

i. *As a prisoner for the Lord, then, I [Paul] urge you to live a life worthy of the calling you have received. Be completely humble and gentle; be patient, bearing with one another in love. Make every effort to keep the unity of the Spirit through the bond of peace. There is one body and one Spirit—just as you were called to one hope when you were called—*[1(B1)b] *one Lord, one faith, one baptism, one God and Father of all, who is over all and through all and in all.*

1 Corinthians 12 [:12-13]

Although Christians are many, they are all one body and live by one Spirit.

ii. *The body is a unit, though it is made up of many parts; and though all its parts are many, they form one body. So it is with Christ. For we were all baptised by one Spirit into one body—whether Jews or Greeks, slave or free—and we were all given the one Spirit to drink.*

Romans 12 [:4-6]

Christians are one body, and each one has his special office and work for the general good of the body, like members in a body.

iii. *Just as each one of us has one body with many members, and these members do not all have the same function, so in Christ we who are many form one body, and each member belongs to all the others. We have different gifts, according to the grace given us.*

1 Corinthians 12 [:18-27]

God appoints each Christian to his own office and activity, of which there must be many sorts, and often those who seem to be the least in the church and to have the worst duty are the most essential members of the body of Christ. The weakest members are to be treated most carefully, and all the members care for one another, sharing together in joy and sadness.

iv. *But in fact God has arranged the parts in the body, every one of them, just as he wanted them to be. If they were all one part, where would the body be? As it is, there are many parts, but one body. The eye cannot say to the hand,* [2(B2)a] *'I don't need you!' And the head cannot say to the feet, 'I don't need you!' On the contrary, those parts of the body that seem to be weaker are indispensable, and the parts that we think are less honourable we treat with special honour. And the parts that are unpresentable are treated with special modesty, while our presentable parts need no special treatment. But God has combined the members of the body and has given greater honour to the parts that lacked it, so that there should be no division in the body, but that its parts should have equal concern for each other. If one part suffers, every part suffers with it; if one part is honoured, every part rejoices with it. Now you are the body of Christ, and each one of you is a part of it.*

[100] Ephesians 4 [:15-16]

Christians grow up into their Head, Christ, being joined and held together one to the other in highest love by means of their appointed calling and service for the general well-being of the body of Christ, that is, the whole congregation.

v. *Instead, speaking the truth in love, we will in all things grow up into him who is the Head, that is, Christ. From him the whole body, joined and held together by every supporting ligament, grows and builds itself up in love, as each part does its work.* [2(B2)b]

Acts 4 [:32,34a,35b]

Christians have their fellowship not only in spiritual matters but also in temporal ones.

vi. *All the believers were one in heart and mind. No-one claimed that any of his possessions was his own, but they shared everything they had . . . There were no needy persons among them . . . it was distributed to anyone as he had need.*

2 Corinthians 8 [:1-5]

Christians dedicate themselves and their possessions to the help of the poor and the promotion of godliness.

vii. *And now, brothers, we want you to know about the grace that God has given the Macedonian churches. Out of the most severe trial, their overflowing joy and their extreme poverty welled up in rich generosity. For I testify that they gave as much as they were able, and even beyond their ability. Entirely on their own, they urgently pleaded with us for the privilege of sharing in this service to the saints. And they did not do as we expected, but they gave themselves first to the Lord and then to us in keeping with God's will.*

2 Corinthians 8 [:13-15]

The sharing of Christians takes place in such a way that those in need are helped and the others not burdened.

viii. *Our desire is not that others might be relieved while you are hard pressed, but that there might be equality. At the present time your plenty will supply their need,* [3(B3)a] *so that in turn their plenty will supply what you need. Then there will be equality, as it is written: 'He who gathered much did not have too much, and he who gathered little did not have too little.'*

2 Thessalonians 3 [:11-13]

Anyone among the Christians who does not want to work and is a burden to other people is not only not to be fed by the congregation, but also to be cast out as one whose way of life is disorderly.

ix. *We hear that some among you are idle. They are not busy; they are busy-bodies. Such people we command and urge in the Lord Jesus Christ to settle down and earn the bread they eat. And as for you, brothers, never tire of doing what is right.*

From these texts we have three things to note. First, how the Christians have such a total and perfect unity among themselves. For because they are one body, partaking of one Spirit, of one calling as being called to one hope and awaiting one salvation, recognizing one Lord, having one faith, all having passed through one baptism, [101] indeed having died and been born again as children of God in Christ, so that they also have only one Father in heaven, they must indeed share together a godly (and therefore the most perfect, kindest and most faithful) brotherhood, fellowship and unity. All this is beautifully expressed by the first [3(B3)b] and second texts. For what fellowship and community could be more united in heart, mind, words and every activity than that which is nothing other than the body of Christ itself, than those who live only by the Spirit of Christ, with no-one seeking his own interests but everyone seeking Christ the Lord alone, when no-one but Christ counts for anything?

The second thing that we have to learn from these texts follows on from the first, and is this: that the fellowship which Christians have with one another is not only the closest and most united, but also the truest and keenest, with everyone demonstrating to the highest degree adroitness and zeal in advising and assisting one another in all things, with everyone regarding the need of others as in the fullest and most real sense his own and taking it to his heart. For however numerous Christians may be, they are still one body, and that the Body of Christ; this means that everyone in Christ is always affected by the feeling of the other, by a genuine Christian feeling, which must be of the heartiest and most active character. The Spirit of Christ is present and effective in each believer, working for the general well-being of the whole body and all its members.

And so every member, because he is a member of Christ and an instrument of the Holy Spirit, is appointed to a particular beneficial work and activity in the body of Christ and endowed with fitness and ability to fulfil that rôle; there is no-one who is idle, no-one who is not constantly [4(B4)a] active for the good of others and also needing the others for his own good. They have various gifts according to the grace which is given them. And the same thing happens with Christians as in the human body: the greater the need, the more they all give themselves to their service and work, whether the need be temporal or spiritual; and this is because each member has his calling which is linked to the other members, [102] through the joints of this divine order and calling.

Moreover the work of all Christians is always geared to the general well-being of the church of Christ, in order that the number of Christians should increase and that those who are already Christians should increase in maturity; and that in every way true godly living should be promoted. As well as in the first two texts all this is clearly and richly set forth in the third, fourth and fifth. All Christians should mark them well and take them to heart.

In the third place, we also have to learn from the above texts that Christians are to look after one another most faithfully not only in spiritual but also in temporal matters, so that no one among them should lack any truly good thing; and so God's command remains which calls some to give and do good, others to receive and profit from the good deeds of others; in this way everyone is cared for in a brotherly manner according to his need, which varies from one to another, and at the same time no-one [4(B4)b] is burdened by others, and no-one profits from the work of others when he does not need to do so. For where the churches of Christ are rightly ordered and have the proper form of government, no toleration is given to anyone who does not want to do anything useful and seeks to live off the labour of others. This is to be seen from the sixth, seventh, eighth and ninth texts.

Thus we have seen from what is set out here what the Christian church, the communion of Christ is, what its extent is, and what its nature and characteristics are: namely, that it is the most united gathering and communion; that its extent is seen in that believers and all the elect are led to Christ the Lord and are built up and provided for, so that they neither lose nor lack any good thing, whether corporal or spiritual, but are constantly led on and encouraged to perfect salvation of body and soul. And all this is provided and achieved for them through various kinds of ministry and gifts.

2

[103] CHRIST'S RULE IN HIS CHURCH

Why there needs to be rule in the church.

Now, because Christians, as long as they live here in this life, never completely divest themselves to be clothed with Christ, never completely die to themselves so that Christ lives in them entirely, but[5(C1)a] still daily err and sin in many ways, it is necessary to have in the church and congregation of Christ a constant teaching, discipline and leading—that is, a rule whereby Christians are continually prompted and led to learn to deny themselves more and abandon and dedicate themselves entirely to Christ the Lord as their Head; so that he may some day live and do his work completely in them, as in his truly living and perfect members.

That Christ alone rules in the church.

This rule in his church is held and led by our Lord Christ personally and by his Spirit. This is why the scripture calls him the King of heaven, the church the kingdom of heaven; him the Master, Christians his disciples and pupils; him the Shepherd, the church his flock; him the Head, Christians his members; him the Bridegroom, the church the bride whom he purifies and cleanses until he presents her to himself as a radiant church without stain or wrinkle; him the Doctor, Christians those who are ill; him the Judge and Bestower of discipline, Christians those who are judged and disciplined. This may be observed from the following texts.

Jeremiah 23 [:5-6]

That Christ himself rules his church. Christ the Lord rules his people in order to make them godly and rich in all good things and safe from all evil.

i. *'The days are coming', declares the Lord, 'when I will raise up to David a righteous Branch, a King who will* [5(C1)b] *reign wisely and do what is just and right in the land. In his days Judah will be saved and Israel will live in safety. This is the name by which he will be called: The Lord Our Righteousness.'*

Luke 1 [:31-33]

Note that Christ must reign eternally in the house of Jacob, i.e. among Christians: his kingdom has no end.

ii. *'You will be with child and give birth to a son, and you are to give him the name Jesus. He will be great and will be called the Son of the Most High. The Lord God will give him the throne of his father David, and he will reign over the house of Jacob for ever; his kingdom will never end.'*

John 17 [:1b-2]

Christ reigns in order to give life eternally, and works in all who belong to his kingdom.

iii. *'Father, the time has come. Glorify your Son, that your Son may glorify you. For you granted him authority over all people that he might give eternal life to all those you have given him.'*

[104] Ephesians 5 [:28b-32]

That Christ is the church's only Bridegroom and Spouse.

iv. *He who loves his wife loves himself. After all, no-one ever hated his own body, but he feeds and cares for it, just* [6(C2)a] *as Christ does the church—for we are members of his body. 'For this reason a man will leave his father and mother and be united to his wife, and the two will become one flesh.' This is a profound mystery—but I am talking about Christ and the church.*

Matthew 23 [:8]

That Christ is the church's only Master and Teacher.

v. *'But you are not to be called "Rabbi", for you have only one Master, Christ.'*

Ezekiel 34 [:11-14]

That the Lord Christ is the only Shepherd of God's sheep, that is, of all God's elect. Note that Christ the Lord himself feeds his sheep, saves them from destruction, and gathers them into his land and feeds them on all the mountains, in all the meadows and pastures of Israel, that is, in all the congregations of Christians.

vi. *'For this is what the Sovereign Lord says: I myself will search for my sheep and look after them. As a shepherd looks after his scattered flock when he is with them, so will I look after my sheep. I will rescue them from all the places where they were scattered on a day of clouds and darkness. I will bring them out from the nations and gather them from the countries, and I will bring them into their own land. I will pasture them on the mountains of Israel, in the ravines and in all the settlements in the land. I will tend them in a good pasture, and the mountain heights of Israel will be their grazing land. There they will lie down in good* [6(C2)b] *grazing land, and there they will feed in a rich pasture on the mountains of Israel.'*

John 10 [:14-15]

Note that Christ the Lord is the only true Good Shepherd, knows his own and his own know him, hear his voice and follow him.

vii. *'I am the good shepherd; I know my sheep and my sheep know me—just as the Father knows me and I know the Father—and I lay down my life for the sheep.'*

Colossians 1 [:18-20]

That Christ the Lord is the only Head of the church.

viii. *And he is the head of the body, the church; he is the beginning and the firstborn from among the dead, so that in everything he might have the supremacy. For God was pleased to have all his fulness dwell in him, and through him to reconcile to himself all things, whether things on earth or things in heaven, by making peace through his blood, shed on the cross.*

John 14 [:23]

That Christ the Lord is always himself present with his church.

ix. *'If anyone loves me, he will obey my teaching. My Father will love him, and we will come to him and make our home with him.'* [7(C3)a]

Matthew 18 [:20]

x. *'For where two or three come together in my name, there am I with them.'*

[105] Matthew 28 [:20b]

xi. *'And surely I am with you always, to the very end of the age.'*

And so we have seen from the aforementioned texts that Christ our Lord alone has and exercises all power and rule in his church and congregation. It is he himself who rules his church, he feeds it, he cares for it, he brings to it those wandering sheep which are still astray; and those which are already in his church he watches over, leads and provides for them, so that they may be daily purified more and more from sins and all the sadness which is brought about by sins, that they may be saved and continually led on and encouraged to grow in piety and blessedness. And the Lord conducts and exercises this rule in the house of Jacob, that is, in the church, eternally; he is and dwells with his people until the end of the world—although not in a tangible sense or in the way of this world, which he has left behind, but nonetheless truly and actually. He acts as a King in his kingdom, a Master with his disciples, a faithful Shepherd with his flock, a Bridegroom with his bride, a Doctor with those who are ill, One who bestows discipline on those who need it. [7(C3)b]

Anyone who does not serve the Lord by means of his word and Christian discipline in his church, but claims that rule for himself, is an antichrist.

Therefore no-one is to claim the Lord's governing authority for himself; for the Lord is never absent from his church, but is always personally present, personally doing and performing everything in all things. This means that all those who claim spiritual authority for themselves over the church of Christ, as the pope and the so-called bishops do, but do not serve the Lord Jesus with the utmost loyalty in providing pasture for these his holy ones, continually encouraging all the elect of God through true faith in him to forsake all their sins and seek all righteousness, by proclaiming the holy gospel and Christian discipline—that is, those who do not share with him in gathering and feeding his lambs, but rather scatter and devastate Christ's sheep—such people are opposed to Christ and have neither part nor share in the kingdom of Christ, that is, in the church of Christ. They are not members of the church, let alone the Lord's governors and administrators; still less [106] should they have any power over the church of Christ to teach and to command, when Christ the Lord has not ordered them to teach and to command.

What the pope and his men are and do in the church.

Now, sadly, it is evident that the pope with all his supposed bishops and church governors are certainly not serving Christ the Lord in rightly giving pasture to his lambs through Christian doctrine and discipline, but instead powerfully setting themselves against all those whom the Lord arouses to serve him in this way. Thus all their power is devoted to public and [8(C4)a] well-known abuses and undeniable distortions of Christian doctrine, the holy sacraments, and all the ordinances of Christ, as they themselves have to admit.

All papists admit that there are many abuses among them, but do not want to do anything to remedy them.

Indeed there is no-one among them who will not acknowledge and confess that the priesthood is in a pitiful state of decay and everything about them is full of abuses. Despite this they are so determined not to allow any place for true Christian reformation and improvement that they allow themselves to be persuaded by advice and action to carry on in those abuses which they themselves acknowledge—may the dear Christ grant that that there may not be hidden away even worse things than are manifest. It is therefore a matter of great concern, unless our faithful chief Shepherd Jesus Christ should parry and turn away their attacks, as he has often graciously and wonderfully done, and they might themselves undertake to feed the lambs of Christ, indeed joining with the sheep and goats in their need to cry out for other shepherds to save them from the wild animals.

Therefore, so long as these poor people do not turn away from their so obvious scattering and spoiling of Christ's lambs to the true service of Christ, they are neither to be considered nor described as Christ's governors or shepherds of Christ's sheep, but rather to be and be called antichrists, that is those who are opposed to Christ; and all their rule over the church is nothing other than what the Lord in John 10 [:1] says of those who do not enter the sheep pen by the gate, but [8(C4)b] climb in by some other way. And the fact that people like this are in control of the church's possessions and, as can be seen, so terribly misuse them, taking for themselves the inheritance of the [107] Crucified and the portion of the poor, is nothing other than what their own canons call it: sacrilege.

This pernicious rape and plundering of Christ's church of its possessions both spiritual and temporal ought to be opposed with the greatest and most urgent seriousness by all princes and rulers, to whom the Lord has appointed and given the highest authority as shepherds of his flock, placing every soul under them, as St Chrysostom comments on this passage of Paul. But let this be done according to true Christian practice and moderation, in such a way that in it nothing other than the authority and rule of Christ is discerned and found; and not that the sacrilege of the priests is just passed over to other people, with the Lord's heritage for his poor and needy servants still being taken away from them. And these shepherds in authority over the people of God must take the greatest care to see that no others claim for themselves any power or rule over Christ's flock, but that there should be and remain in the church none other than the sole power and absolute authority of Christ, who is to be faithfully served by all who are chosen to the care of souls and pastoral office in the [9(D1)a] church. This is what we are constantly to pray for when we pray: *Your kingdom come* (Matt. 6:10a).

3

THE MANAGEMENT OF THE CHURCH: HOW OUR LORD JESUS CARRIES OUT HIS PASTORAL OFFICE AND THE WORK OF OUR SALVATION IN HIS CHURCH THROUGH HIS ORDAINED MINISTERS

As we have already said, our dear Lord Jesus is truly present in his church, ruling, leading, and feeding it himself. But he effects and carries out this his rule and the feeding of his lambs in such a way as to remain always in his heavenly nature, that is, in his divine and intangible state, because he has left this world. Therefore it has pleased him to exercise his rule, protection and care of us who are still in this world with and through the ministry of his word, [108] which he does outwardly and tangibly through his ministers and instruments. This we discover from the following texts.

Matthew 28 [:18-20]

Note that the apostles are to make disciples for the Lord, and baptize people, that is, those who are born again, and are then to teach them everything that he has commanded. In this way people are made holy.

i. *'All authority in heaven and on earth has been given to me. Therefore go and make disciples of all nations, baptising them in the name of the Father and of the Son and of the* [9(D1)b] *Holy Spirit, and teaching them to obey everything I have commanded you. And surely I am with you always, to the very end of the age.'*

Luke 24 [:45-47]

Note that the Lord makes his servants learned in the Scriptures, so that they can preach repentance and forgiveness of sins, that is, bring people salvation.

ii. *Then he opened their minds so they could understand the Scriptures. He told them, 'This is what is written: The Christ will suffer and rise from the dead on the third day, and repentance and forgiveness of sins will be preached in his name to all nations, beginning at Jerusalem.'*

John 15 [:16]

Note that the Lord has ordained his ministers of the Word, so that they might obtain a lasting fruit among people, that is, their salvation.

iii. *'You did not choose me, but I chose you and appointed you to go and bear fruit—fruit that will last. Then the Father will give you whatever you ask in my name.'*

John 20 [:21-23]

Note how our Lord has been sent by the Father, and in the same way sends his ministers, gives them his Spirit and authority to forgive and retain sins, that is, to accept for salvation or reject for damnation.

iv. *Again Jesus said, 'Peace be with you! As the Father has sent me, I am sending you.' And with that he breathed on them and said, 'Receive the Holy Spirit. If you forgive anyone his sins, they are* [10(D2)a] *forgiven; if you do not forgive them, they are not forgiven.'*

Matthew 16 [:19]

The Lord wishes to open and close access to heaven through the agency of his ministers.

> v. *'I will give you the keys of the kingdom of heaven: whatever you bind on earth will be bound in heaven, and whatever you loose on earth will be loosed in heaven.'*

Matthew 10 [:20]

Note that the Holy Spirit speaks in the apostles.

> vi. *'It will not be you speaking, but the Spirit of your Father speaking through you.'*

1 Corinthians 3 [:5-7]

Note that people come to faith through the ministers of Christ, although the work is certainly of God.

> vii. *What, after all, is Paul? And what is Apollos? Only servants, through whom you came to believe—as the Lord has assigned to each his task. [109] I planted the seed, Apollos watered it, but God made it grow. So neither he who plants nor he who waters is anything, but only God, who makes things grow.*

1 Corinthians 4 [:1]

> viii. *So then, men ought to regard us as servants of Christ and as those entrusted with the secret things of God.* [10(D2)b]

2 Corinthians 3 [:2-6]

Note that the Lord uses his ministers to inscribe himself upon people's hearts, imparting to them not only the letter but the Spirit, and through them establishes the New Testament, the New Covenant of the grace of eternal life.

> ix. *You yourselves are our letter, written on our hearts, known and read by everybody. You show that you are a letter from Christ, the result of our ministry, written not with ink but with the Spirit of the living God, not on tablets of stone but on tablets of human hearts. Such confidence as this is ours through Christ before God. Not that we are competent in ourselves to claim anything for ourselves, but our competence comes from God. He has made us competent as ministers of a new covenant—not of the letter but of the Spirit; for the letter kills, but the Spirit gives life.*

1 Thessalonians 1 [:4-5]

Note that Paul's preaching was with power and with the Holy Spirit.

> x. *For we know, brothers loved by God, that he has chosen you, because our gospel came to you not simply with words, but also with power, with the Holy Spirit and with deep conviction. You know how we lived among you for your sake.*

1 Thessalonians 2 [:13] [11(D3)A]

Paul's preaching was the word of God, not of a man.

> xi. *And we also thank God continually because, when you received the word of God, which you heard from us, you accepted it not as the word of men, but as it actually is, the word of God, which is at work in you who believe.*

The Lord makes people Christians and saves them through the church's ministry.

From the above-mentioned texts we can see very clearly and obviously that our Lord Jesus, now in his heavenly nature, is with us and rules and feeds us from heaven; this rule and feeding, that is, the work of our salvation, he exercises among us through his ministers, whom he calls, ordains and uses for that purpose. Through them he calls all nations to reformation and declares to them forgiveness of sins, pardoning their sins and accepting them as his disciples, giving them new birth [110] to godly life in holy baptism and then teaching them all their lives long to keep everything that he has commanded them. This is shown by the first, second, fourth and fifth texts.

The work of the church's ministry is necessary for the Lord to work in man's heart and innermost being.

And in all this these ministers of the church are *servants of Christ and stewards of the secret things of God* [1 Cor. 4:1], that is, of Christ's salvation and of the Holy Spirit, not merely of the letter. They take the elect of God and raise them up into the new eternal covenant which has been established through the blood of our Lord Jesus Christ with all God's elect throughout the whole world. They also serve [11(D3)b] the Lord in ministering the holy gospel to his elect, teaching and admonishing them and also administering the holy sacraments, so that people might come to him, Christ our Lord, and be saved, as indicated by the third, seventh, eighth and ninth of our texts.

The power and work of the church's ministry belongs not to the ministers, but to Christ the Lord.

But this they certainly do not accomplish by their own powers, but through the power and work of the Lord. Of themselves they could not even think of doing such a thing, but God equips them for the ministry, to that end the Lord gives them his Spirit and understanding of the Scriptures, his Spirit speaks through them, it is his power, his Spirit and his work, it is he who gives success. To this the first, second, fourth, sixth, seventh, ninth, tenth and eleventh texts bear witness.

The pernicious error of those who regard the church's ministry as insignificant and invalid.

From this we must go on to learn how harmful and pernicious those people are who teach that this ministry of the church is of no importance, a merely outward activity which does not contribute in any particular way to our salvation, and without which it is quite possible to become a Christian and receive God's gifts. The Lord, they say, must inwardly teach his own, washing and purifying them, giving them new birth, feeding and strengthening them and leading them on in all good things. The truth, on the other hand, says that the Lord must indeed do and effect all this alone and by himself, and not only inwardly but also outwardly; because if the word and the sacrament which we outwardly hear and receive are not the word, sacrament and work of Christ, then they are the word, sacrament and work of the antichrist and Satan. There is no middle ground here.

[12(D4)a] But St Paul and all the apostles, together with all genuine Christian ministers, maintain and wish it to be recognized, held and accepted that in this ministry they are certainly not dispensing their own word or signs. Nor are they those who speak or act or work on their own account, but rather they are those who dispense the word and secret things [111] of God and do the work of Christ. In their ministry they want people to look not at themselves, but at Christ the Lord, and therefore they want to be and be recognized not as ministers of the letter, that is, of outward activity, but of the Spirit, through whom they bring people to faith and thus to salvation, writing Christ upon their hearts. The faithful apostle expresses and testifies to this so diligently in the seventh, eighth, ninth and eleventh of our texts. All power and the whole work in this matter belong to Christ our dear Lord; but ministers are his instruments, through whom he effects and fulfils this work of his in his elect.

This is why in old times the children of God had to be instructed in and admitted to salvation through the ministry of the holy fathers by means of circumcision. It was through Moses that even the high priest Aaron and all the people of God had to enter into God's covenant and service. As soon as the Lord called apostles, it was their duty to lead the others and all the children of God to the Lord. God sent an angel to Cornelius to declare his grace to him, but he still had to be properly [12(D4)b] taught and given new birth through St Peter [Acts 10]. Christ himself converted Paul from heaven, but he still had to be taught more fully through Ananias and washed and purified from his sins through baptism [Acts 9:1-19; 22:3-16]. So the Lord simply wants to maintain this order whereby he performs the work of our conversion, redemption and the whole of salvation in us through his ministers. The first of those ministers he called himself, the others he calls, ordains and appoints through the ministry of his church.

This is why all pious Christians should use the texts we have set out to guard themselves against the wholly pernicious error which despises the church's ministry of word and sacrament as a superficial and unnecessary thing, and would have everything given and received from Christ in heaven without using the means which the Lord himself desires to employ. And they should oppose all those who introduce this error with these words: 'I wish to maintain the order of my Lord, who ordains in his church his appointed ministers, through whom it is his will to gather me into his kingdom, to pardon my sins, to give me new birth, to keep me, teach me, and lead me to eternal life. I intend to listen to them and their word and work in this ministry as to the Lord himself, so long as they exercise their ministry according to the Lord's appointment, not as their own word and work but as the word and work [112] of my Lord Jesus Christ which they truly are, hearing and receiving them so that they may work in me too, to the praise of the Lord and the salvation of his elect.' [13(E1)a]

4

THE VARIOUS MINISTERS OUR LORD JESUS HAS AND USES IN HIS CHURCH

The miracle-working ministers in the kingdom of Christ, whom the Lord used only at the commencement of the church.

Thus our dear Lord Jesus exercises his rule in his church by calling everyone to it and ensuring that those who commit themselves to his church lack no good thing, either in spiritual or in temporal matters. This is why from the commencement of the church he has not only appointed and used one sort of minister to bring about the salvation of his people. There are some whom he used only at the beginning, to awaken the world to his word and kingdom, such as prophets, who had the gift to declare those things which were hidden or in the future. Similarly those to whom he gave the gift of speaking immediately in many and foreign languages, and those who performed miracles and had the gift of bringing healing by calling on his name.

What apostles are.

There are other ministries which the Lord still uses today, but not in so general or powerful a way as in the commencement of the church. Thus the apostles who bring the kingdom of Christ from one place to another, as the Lord's chief legates and ambassadors: at the beginning these spread the kingdom of Christ far and wide in a short time, setting up churches in every place. It may be that the Lord still provides this sort of ministry today and at all times, but we do not have so many of them, nor do they maintain in their apostolate so powerful a spirit and so exalted [13(E1)b] a rôle as the first apostles did.

The ordinary ministers of the church are pastors, teachers, and those ministering to the poor.

The ordinary ministers whom the Lord gives to his church all the time are pastors, teachers, and those ministers commissioned by the whole church to care for those in need. These are indicated to us by the following texts; and first:—

The Ministry of Teaching and Spiritual Discipline

1 Corinthians 12 [:28]

God himself places ministers in his church, both apostles and others, including teachers, helpers, and governors.

i. *In the church God has appointed first of all apostles, second prophets, third teachers, then workers of miracles, also those having gifts of healing, those able to help others, those with gifts of administration, and those speaking in different kinds of tongues.*

[113] Ephesians 4 [:11-12]

Christ himself places all ministers in his congregation, including pastors and teachers, so that through their ministry the church should be built up in the word and discipline.

ii. *It was he who gave some to be apostles, some to be prophets, some to be evangelists, and some to be pastors and teachers, to prepare God's people for works of service, so that the body of Christ may be built up.*

26

Titus 1 [:5-6]

Note that the Holy Spirit wishes to have elders in each congregation to exercise the episcopal ministry.

[14(E2)a] iii. *The reason I left you in Crete was that you might straighten out what was left unfinished and appoint elders in every town, as I directed you. An elder must be blameless, the husband of but one wife, a man whose children believe and are not open to the charge of being wild and disobedient.*

Acts 15 [:2b]

The first church at Jerusalem, appointed by Christ and the Holy Spirit to be an example to all churches, also had its elders as well as the apostles.

iv. *So Paul and Barnabas were appointed, along with some other believers, to go up to Jerusalem to see the apostles and elders about this question.*

Acts 15 [:22a]

With everything in the church the advice of the elders was taken into account.

v. *And it seemed good to the apostles and elders, with the whole church.*

Acts 15 [:23b]

vi. *The apostles and elders and brothers, to the Gentile believers . . . Greetings.*

Acts 14 [:21b-23]

Because it is necessary for the church to have its elders so that they may be established in the faith through the daily ministry of the word, Paul and Barnabas have also placed elders in these churches. And no doubt they had the confidence and high regard of these churches.

vii. *Paul and Barnabas returned to Lystra, Iconium and Antioch, strengthening the disciples and encouraging them to remain true to the faith. 'We must go through many hardships [14(E2)b] to enter the kingdom of God', they said. Paul and Barnabas appointed elders for them in every church and, with prayer and fasting, committed them to the Lord, in whom they had put their trust.*

Acts 20 [:17, 28]

The Holy Spirit places elders in the churches and desires them to be bishops, that is, applying and providing the care of souls in every respect.

viii. *From Miletus, Paul sent to Ephesus for the elders of the church. And to these he said amongst other things: Keep watch over yourselves and all the flock of which the Holy Spirit has made you bishops. Be shepherds of the church of God.*

Acts 21 [:18]

James was the foremost among the other elders and the chief bishop. This is why Paul went to him first, and the other elders also went to him.

ix. *The next day Paul and the rest of us went to see James, and all the elders came.*

THE MINISTRY TO THE NEEDS OF THE BODY

[114] Acts 6 [:1-6]

There are two sorts of ministry, and they are to be shared between different people: the ministry of the word and discipline, and the ministry of temporal care for those in need.

The local church elects them, choosing those who are gifted with the Holy Spirit and wisdom and adorned with good reputation.

The apostles confirm the choice and install those who have been chosen into office with the laying-on of hands, that is, imparting to them the assistance of the Holy Spirit in their office.

> i. *In those days when the number of the disciples was increasing, the Grecian Jews among them complained against the Hebraic Jews because their widows were being overlooked* [15E3)a] *in the daily distribution of food. So the Twelve gathered all the disciples together and said, 'It would not be right for us to neglect the ministry of the word of God in order to wait on tables. Brothers, choose seven men from among you who are known to be full of the Spirit and wisdom. We will turn this responsibility over to them and will give our attention to prayer and the ministry of the word.' This proposal pleased the whole group. They chose Stephen, a man full of faith and of the Holy Spirit; also Philip, Procorus, Nicanor, Timon, Parmenas, and Nicolas from Antioch, a convert to Judaism. They presented these men to the apostles, who prayed and laid their hands on them.*

1 Timothy 3 [:8-10]

Even those who minister in the church only in temporal matters are nonetheless to be entirely blameless and holy in the sight of others.

> ii. *Deacons, likewise, are to be men worthy of respect, sincere, not indulging in much wine, and not pursuing dishonest gain. They must keep*

hold of the deep truths of the faith with a clear conscience. They must
first be tested, and then if there is nothing against them, let them serve
as deacons.

[15(E3)b] From these texts we learn that the general oversight of the church at all times consists primarily in these two ministries: the ministry of the care of souls, and the ministry to the body of those in need.

What deacons, archdeacons and subdeacons are.

Those who are appointed to this ministry of bodily care, for as long as this office has been practised in the church, the apostles and the church after them have named deacons, i.e. servants. And as the church increased and spread there were also appointed subdeacons, i.e. under-servants, and then archdeacons, i.e. arch- or over-servants.

The ministry of the deacons is the providing of alms.

What this office and ministry was and should still be is this: to take faithful charge, both at home and on the move, of what Christians bring and offer for the care of the poor at their assemblies on Sundays and at other times, and also what particular people, whether of high or low standing, give to the church for this work of God; and to distribute it to all the needy in the congregation, both local people and visitors, according to the general rule of the church and also the particular instructions of the elders and especially of the chief pastor, i.e. the bishop. This is because the bishop, as the chief overseer of all need in the [115] church, and the elders as his fellow-overseers, are aware of the daily occurring need of Christians, strangers and local alike, and observe the help that can be given to them according to the church's resources.

[16(E4)a] And these ministers of the church have always kept faithful account of the income and expenditure of the church's assets, as can be clearly seen from the ancient holy fathers and the church laws or canons. This is shown particularly well in the epistles of St Gregory, who was a pious pope of Rome.

But this office and ministry have for a long time been so subjugated to popish tyranny in the church, and sadly completely fallen into decay, that for many years now there are few even of those who are called deacons, subdeacons and archdeacons who know what their office or ministry in the church should be, although they enjoy so great a use of these offices. They think that all they have to do is to sing the gospel or the epistle at the mass or arrange for it to be sung. Sadly, all the church's assets have long since been completely taken away from it by our so-called priests, and so misappropriated and misused that the whole of Christendom must to the highest degree fear before God and be ashamed before the world. For these people themselves call these assets the inheritance of the Crucified and the portion of the church, which should be applied and used only for the maintenance of the needy and the building up of the kingdom of God among men, as the canons overwhelmingly demonstrate.

When the so-called priests took the church's assets away from the poor, the pious wanted to replace them by other charitable foundations, but then the priests squandered these as well.

In earlier times pious Christians have wanted to make up to some measure for this sacrilege and harm done to poor Christians by the so-called priests, by setting up all sorts of alms-houses, orphanages and infirmaries. [16(E4)b] But once the supposed priests used the authority they claimed to get these alms-houses and foundations also into their clutches, they long ago turned the majority of these alms-houses and foundations also into places for prelates and splendour, monasteries and houses: as you can see from those hospitals dedicated to the Holy Spirit, the virgin Mary, St John and other saints.

[116] Indeed, the same thing happened in days gone by with the older houses of God, that is, the old foundations and monasteries, which were all intended for the care of the poor and those who were to be educated and supported for the ministry of the church. Instead, through the cunning and violence of the antichrist they have been devoted to the mischief and splendour of his followers rather than to the service of the church of Christ.

General almsgiving as it is presently organized is only a beginning of the proper care of all the needy, as it should be in the church.

Now that the Lord has at this time granted us a more perfect understanding of his word, arrangements have again been made in the churches for the general care of the poor; but in this as in almost every other aspect of Christian reformation, we have made a mere beginning when compared with what is required by Christian love and true zeal for the kingdom of Christ, and we can see the example of Christians of old, in what is still sacrilegiously retained in the hands of the papists. Therefore this ministry should be reintroduced, whereby everyone should be concerned about people's needs in such a way that he wishes to use his own possessions for the sake of Christ's kingdom, and no one should suffer lack, [17(F1)a] as we have before us the example of the first church in Acts 4 [:32ff.].

That is enough to say here concerning the ministry and office through which the Lord wishes to provide in his church for the bodily needs of his people. More is to be said concerning the office and ministry of the care of souls: for where the office of the care of souls is properly ordered and practised, we will not expect to see anything much lacking in this other ministry of care to the body.

The end and goal of the pastoral office.

It is through this ministry that all the elect of God, whom the Father has given to him, our Lord Christ, but have not yet been brought into the church, that is, his sheep-pen, will one day be brought into the church and his sheep-pen and incorporated into our Lord. And those who have already been brought into the church and his communion are not only [117] kept there, but also absolved from all their sins and led and encouraged in all that is good, that they might constantly increase in godliness and grow to a perfect man in Christ, so that both in understanding and in life [17(F1)b] no-one should be lacking. That is the purpose and goal of the pastoral office in the church, as we will further prove.

Now all this is to be achieved and attained solely through teaching, exhorting, warning, disciplining, comforting, pardoning, and reconciling to the Lord and his church: in other words the proclaiming of the whole word of God. And it requires a suitable and noble reputation and a necessary sense of awe, along with that good example of life which those who exercise the pastoral office are to display to the flock. We will further introduce texts on this matter.

The churches need to have many exercising the pastoral ministry if it is to be properly carried out.

Because so much is involved in the pastoral office, with teaching, exhortation, warning and discipline, comfort and pardon; and for this a reputation, a sense of awe, and an example of life are required; and since the whole of this so varied ministry has to be carried out in such a way as to help any and every one of the elect; every Christian can easily see how various kinds of exalted gifts and skills are needed, as well as all the earnest zeal, for the proper execution of the pastoral office. This is because the people who are to be won for the Lord, preserved and built up in him, are not all of one sort and have many and various weaknesses, and also the number of people in the churches is large. Therefore the Lord also gives to each one his own gifts and task, not all the gifts to one or two, but will rather that always one should need and make use of the help of another.

The Lord shares among many the gifts necessary for the pastoral office.

To one he gives the skill of teaching clearly and understandably, [18(F2)a] while not endowing him with so much grace in exhorting; to another he gives ability to exhort warmly and seriously, without also enabling him to be powerful in the teaching and exposition of the scriptures. To another he grants an especially effective enthusiasm in chastising and disciplining, though he may not be able to achieve much in either teaching or exhorting. One the Lord has endowed with a fine upright and honest spirit to care for the whole congregation and to provide timely provision and protection where Satan wants to break in, while he does not have great abilities otherwise, either in teaching or exhorting. There are those whom the Lord has appointed to exercise their ministry conscientiously and usefully to the bruised and wounded, warmly and [118] powerfully comforting them and applying the right measure of gravity and discipline, but who are not particularly effective in other aspects of the pastoral office.

The churches need a good number of elders.

Therefore, since the pastoral office involves such a great and important work, and one which so long as we live here is unending, that of presenting the church of Christ in all its members without fault, without stain or wrinkle, this office requires many sorts of ministry and work. As we have already said, we intend to introduce further texts concerning both these matters. And since the Lord has also bestowed and distributed the gifts necessary for this office not to one or two, but in different ways to many, it was his will that his churches, if they were able to have meetings and essential order, should have elders, whether few or many, according to the requirement [18(F2)b] of each congregation. These elders are necessary for the work we have referred to, that of winning and building up all those who belong to such a congregation, whether they are already coming to it or are yet to be brought. All the aforementioned texts following the first and second testify to this.

It is through none other than the Holy Spirit that St Paul commanded Titus to appoint elders in the towns in Crete. Similarly the first church in Jerusalem, to which the Holy Spirit was given with visible signs and which church the apostles themselves governed, did not choose and appoint their elders without the assistance of the Holy Spirit.

The fact that there should be a considerable number of elders, according to the requirements of each church, can be recognized from the great and far-reaching nature of the work and ministry of the pastoral office; but from the third and seventh texts it can also be seen that this is the Lord's rule. At Ephesus the Holy Spirit placed several elders as bishops, not just one. So it was that St Paul commanded that several elders should be appointed in all the towns in Crete, not just one, although the churches in the towns of this island at that time certainly consisted of quite small numbers of people.

The elders exercise the whole pastoral office.

But the fact that in apostolic times such elders were entrusted with the whole pastoral office and all its duties can be sufficiently learned from all the above texts, and *[119]* most expressly in [19(F3)a] the third and seventh. From the same third text we can also see that the apostle orders that these elders should be bishops. He has established that Titus is to appoint elders to the towns, and such elders as were blameless: in order to add a reason for this he says,

For a bishop must be blameless [Titus 1:7]. It is as if he wanted to say: The reason I require elders who are blameless is because these elders are to be bishops, that is, general overseers, and shepherds of the Christians. The episcopal office requires that they should be blameless; because those who are to minister to all the others in order that they should live blameless and holy lives must of necessity themselves be more holy, blameless and free of all reproach than any others.

From this it can be clearly seen that the apostle here means elders who will be bishops, that is, the proper overseers, carers of souls, and shepherds of the flock of Christ. That is why it is the Holy Spirit's rule that each church should have several elders, who are all shepherds and bishops, that is, overseers to carry out the care of souls and the pastoral office.

This can be observed even more clearly in the seventh text. Because when St Luke tells us how St Paul called the elders of the church at Ephesus to join him at Miletus and then recounts the speech that the apostle gave to them, he writes that the apostle said to these elders among other things: *Keep watch over yourselves and all the flock of which the Holy Spirit* [19(F3)b] *has made you bishops, to feed the church of God* [Acts 20:28].

Note that the Holy Spirit has made these elders, as the apostle testifies, bishops, to feed the church of God. They were to be the chief overseers and shepherds of the flock of Christ. Thus we find repeatedly that according to the rule of the Holy Spirit the general care of souls and pastoral office is to be laid upon all the elders of the church. This is why St Jerome rightly decided that the office of elders and bishops is one office and one order.

There has however been a presiding elder who was particularly referred to as bishop.

However, St Jerome goes on to write that at the beginning of the church such elders gave general counsel to the churches and ruled them [120] but then one of the elders was set over the others and given the special title of bishop, since sects and groups were beginning to emerge in the church and everyone wanted to have his own group attached to him. But this was not a long-standing practice, not was it the case in all churches; for we have clear evidence from more ancient fathers than St Jerome that in all the most prominent churches from the time of the apostles the elders were all entrusted with the episcopal office. However, even in the apostles' time one of the elders was chosen and ordained as a superior in this office, presiding over all the others and bearing and carrying out to the furthest and highest degree the care of souls and episcopal office.

[20(F4)a] In the same way the rule in the first church at Jerusalem is presented to us: for St Luke describes James as presiding over the whole congregation and all the elders; in the fifteenth chapter [13ff.] of Acts he recounts how in the council of the church after Peter it is James who speaks before all the elders; and he writes about dear Paul that when he came to Jerusalem for the last time and had to report to the church there concerning his ministry, he first went to James and then the elders came to join them, as indicated by the eighth *[ninth]* text above. The same order was also perpetually maintained in other churches, as far as we can tell from the evidence of church history, and also all the most ancient fathers, such as Tertullian, Cyprian, Irenæus, Eusebius, and others. And this is also required by the human need that whenever there are matters in which many people are involved, one or perhaps a few need to be appointed to preside over the others, speaking and acting on their behalf. This is to be seen in all political situations: the government may be entirely by common consent, with authority lying with the whole community, but still there will be one or two leading citizens responsible for presiding over and dealing with all the matters of government; but they do this not on their own authority, but according to the common rule and with the recognition of the whole council. It is these chief citizens alone who have the chief responsibility for making known the needs of government, giving and seeking advice, [20(F4)b] and according to the decision of the majority informing, ordering and acting; but all for the sake of and in the name [121] of the whole council and the city in general, not for their own sake or on their own authority.

So this is how also elders in the church are to be, and consider themselves to be, in carrying out their office and ministry of the care of souls. They are all to be faithful in caring and striving so that the kingdom of Christ might increase in all and Christ's lambs be well pastured.

But in order that this might proceed in an orderly and productive way such elders in the church of God have, as we have shown, chosen and appointed either from among themselves or from others a president who, like the chief citizens in towns, has borne the greatest responsibility for the church and had the chief oversight over all the ministry and business carried out by the church. He has also had the greatest rôle in providing Christian teaching, exhortation and discipline on behalf of the church in general and on the advice of the elders. On account of this chief oversight this one has been called the bishop, that is, overseer or supervisor.

Résumé of this article concerning what ministers the Lord uses in his church. The churches are to have their elders, as many in number as the needs of each church require; and among them one who is bishop and chief elder.

So now we see how there are various sorts of ministry which the Lord generally and at all times uses in his church, in order that his people may be properly shepherded and cared for, so that they lack no good thing and are preserved from all trouble. Therefore all properly ordered churches of Christ are provided with such ministers. They will have their elders to exercise the [21(G1)a] care of souls and pastoral ministry, as many as are required by the need of each church, depending on the number of people in it and the circumstances of the church. And among these elders the rule of the Holy Spirit will also be maintained, whereby a few have the major responsibility and chief oversight over the flock of Christ, lest as the popular proverb has it, many shepherds mean poor care. In addition the ministry of care of the body in such churches through the ministers ordained for that purpose will be arranged and carried out in such a way that no-one suffers lack, but also no-one lives disorderly and is a burden to others. Now we want [122] to see by whom and how these elders are to be chosen and ordained by the churches and presiding elders.

5

WHAT SORT OF PEOPLE THE ELDERS ARE TO BE, AND HOW THEY ARE TO BE CHOSEN AND INSTALLED

That the ministers of the church must be well trusted and loved in the congregation and skilled and zealous in the service of the church.

Since these servants of the Lord are to fulfil the work of our salvation in the church by means of teaching, exhorting, warning, chastising, disciplining, pardoning, and all this through the dispensing of God's word, as we want to set out further here from the testimony of Scripture, and at the same time people are weak and discipline and punishment are unpleasant, it is necessary that these ministers should as much as possible [21(G1)b] be trusted and respected by the believers among whom they are to serve the Lord, and also that they be possessed of a genuine zeal to be faithful shepherds of Christ's sheep, and equipped with the requisite skills and the power of the Holy Spirit. This is why the greatest fear of God and the most earnest diligence are to be employed in the choice and installation of such men.

This is what we have to learn from the following texts. However, anyone can infer this by himself from a right comparison of the order of elders with the character and nature of our being.

1 Timothy 3 [:1-12]

Those chosen for the ministry of the church are to be of a good reputation with believers and unbelievers alike, holy in their personal lives, faithful towards their neighbours, adorned with every virtue; powerful in teaching, exhortation, and refutation of false doctrine, skilled in managing and giving evidence of that in their own families.

i. *Here is a trustworthy saying: If anyone sets his heart on being a bishop, he desires a noble task. Now the bishop must be above reproach, the husband of but one wife, temperate, self-controlled, respectable, hospitable, able to teach, not given to drunkenness, not violent but gentle, not quarrelsome, not a lover of money. He must manage his own family well and see that his children obey him with proper respect. (If anyone does not know how to manage his own family, how can he take care of God's church?) He must not be a recent convert, or he may become conceited and fall under the same judgment as the devil. He must also have a good reputation with outsiders, so that he will not fall into disgrace and into the devil's trap. Deacons, likewise,* [22(G2)a] *are to be men worthy of respect, sincere, not indulging in much wine, and not pursuing dishonest gain. They must keep hold of the deep truths of the faith with a clear conscience. They must first be tested;* [12] *and then if there is nothing against them, let them serve as deacons. In the same way, their wives are to be women worthy of respect, not malicious talkers but temperate and trustworthy in everything. A deacon must be the husband of but one wife and must manage his children and his household well.*

Titus 1 [:5-9]

Titus was to appoint the elders from such people as those described to Timothy, and also on the basis of the testimonial and choice of the believers.

ii. *The reason I left you in Crete was that you might straighten out what was left unfinished and appoint elders in every town, as I directed you. An elder must be blameless, the husband of but one wife, a man whose children believe and are not open to the charge of being wild and disobedient. Since a bishop is entrusted with God's work, he must be blameless—not overbearing, not quick-tempered, not given to drunkenness, not violent, not pursuing dishonest gain. Rather he must be hospitable, one who loves what is good, who is self-controlled, upright, holy and disciplined. He must hold firmly to the trustworthy message as it has been taught, so that he can encourage others by sound doctrine and refute those who oppose it.*[22(G2)b]

2 Timothy 2 [:1-10]

Those are to be chosen for the church's ministry who are faithful and competent to teach others also, who can endure hardship in Christ's battle, and have completely renounced the concern and business of temporal affairs.

iii. *You then, my son, be strong in the grace that is in Christ Jesus. And the things you have heard me say in the presence of many witnesses entrust to reliable men who will also be qualified to teach others. Endure hardship with us like a good soldier of Christ Jesus. No-one serving as a soldier gets involved in civilian affairs—he wants to please his commanding officer. Similarly, if anyone competes as an athlete, he does not receive the victor's crown unless he competes according to the rules. The hardworking farmer should be the first to receive a share of the crops. Reflect on what I am saying, for the Lord will give you insight into all this. Remember Jesus Christ, raised from the dead, descended from David. This is my gospel, for which I am suffering even to the point of being chained like a criminal. But God's word is not chained. Therefore I endure everything for the sake of the elect, that they too may obtain the salvation that is in Christ Jesus, with eternal glory.*

2 Timothy 2 [:15-17a]

The ministers of the church must be skilled and experienced, and also well proven in their correct handling of the word of God and guarding against false doctrine.

iv. *Do your best to present yourself to God as one approved, a workman who does not need to be ashamed and who* [23(G3)a] *correctly handles the word of truth. Avoid godless chatter, because those who indulge in it will become more and more ungodly. Their teaching will spread like gangrene.*

2 Timothy 2 [:22-26]

Those who are to be chosen for the ministry of the church must strictly avoid the lusts of the flesh and pursue all virtue, have nothing to do with presumptuous or impudent questions, be not quarrelsome but kind to everyone and patient with those who are bad, and skilful in the effective exposition and steadfast defence of Christian doctrine.

v. *Flee the evil desires of youth, and pursue righteousness, faith, love and peace, along with those who call on the Lord out of a pure heart. Don't have anything to do with foolish and stupid arguments, because you know they produce quarrels. And the Lord's servant must not quarrel; instead, he must be kind to everyone, able to teach, not resentful. Those who oppose him he must gently instruct, in the hope that God will grant them repentance leading them to a knowledge of the truth, and* [124] *that they will come to their senses and escape from the trap of the devil, who has taken them captive to do his will.*

2 Timothy 3 [:14-17]

Those are to be chosen to the highest position among the elders who, as Timothy was, have been taught in the holy scriptures from infancy.

> vi. *But as for you, continue in what you have learned and have become convinced of, because you know those from whom you learned it, and how from infancy you have known the holy Scriptures, which are able to make you wise for salvation through faith in Christ* [23(G3)b] *Jesus. All Scripture is God-breathed and is useful for teaching, rebuking, correcting and training in righteousness, so that the man of God may be thoroughly equipped for every good work.*

1 Timothy 4 [:12-16]

Those are to be chosen for the ministry of the church who are not to be despised, and in cases where because of their youth they might be valued less highly, they are to earn their reputation through the excellence of their doctrine and life. Note how the church's ministers are to be chosen, and that the gift of the Holy Spirit to fulfil the ministry well is bestowed with the laying-on of hands of the elders. Note also that hands are laid only on those who are constantly marked out by the Holy Spirit working in them, as Timothy was marked out by the prophetic message.

> vii. *Don't let anyone look down on you because you are young, but set an example for the believers in speech, in life, in love, in faith and in purity. Until I come, devote yourself to the public reading of Scripture, to preaching and to teaching. Do not neglect your gift, which was given you through a prophetic message when the body of elders laid their hands on you. Be diligent in these matters; give yourself wholly to them, so that everyone may see your progress. Watch your life and doctrine closely. Persevere in them, because if you do, you will save both yourself and your hearers.*

1 Timothy 5 [:21-22b]

How the ministers of the church are to be chosen with such great diligence and no-one is lightly to have hands laid on him, i.e. no-one is to be accepted untried into this ministry.

> viii. *I charge you, in the sight of God and Christ Jesus and the elect angels, to keep these instructions without partiality, and to do nothing out of favouritism. Do not be hasty in the laying on of hands,* [24(G4)a] *and do not share in the sins of others.*

Acts 13 [:1-3]

That in choosing ministers we are to be diligent in seeking the choice of the Holy Spirit, that he might reveal to us what we have been carefully considering and diligently praying for; and with what seriousness and devotion they are to be appointed by all the churches.

> ix. *In the church at Antioch there were prophets and teachers: Barnabas, Simeon called Niger, Lucius of Cyrene, Manaen (who had been brought up with Herod the tetrarch) and Saul. While they were worshipping the Lord and fasting, the Holy Spirit said, 'Set apart for me Barnabas and Saul for the work to which I have called them.' So after they had fasted and prayed, they placed their hands on them and sent them off.*

From these texts we learn that the church's ministers are to be chosen from those who are, firstly, blameless in the sight of all, with a good reputation as far as they themselves, and also their wives, children and servants are concerned. This is demonstrated by the first and second texts.

Secondly, those who have a good reputation and are recognized and deemed to be suitable and powerful in teaching and government: the third and fourth texts teach this.

Thirdly, those who are adorned with all virtues beyond others: this is shown by the first, second, fifth and seventh texts.

[125] [24(G4)b] But it is a special requirement of the Holy Spirit that they should excel in those virtues by which they may be a particularly outstanding example to the flock of Christ: the virtues of all holiness as far as they themselves are concerned, and all justice towards their neighbours; and also that in teaching, chastising, and all the work of the pastoral office they show themselves to be very skilled, zealous, kind and loving, so that they may the better win people and build up those who have been won.

What discipline and holiness are required in the ministers of the church.

In the first place it is the will of the Holy Spirit that the church's ministers should each be the husband of only one wife, temperate, virtuous, well-mannered, holy, self-controlled, pure, not addicted to wine. They should be able to maintain discipline, so that no charge of indiscipline can be laid against their own children and servants. In other words, it is the will of the Holy Spirit that such people should demonstrate in themselves and in those who belong to them the highest degree of discipline and holiness, and complete renunciation of all fleshly lusts and concerns.

This is because if they are to teach the whole church to renounce all fleshly desires and lusts it is necessary for them to furnish the highest example of this in themselves and those who belong to them. And those who do not stand earnestly and firmly against things of this nature will easily be overtaken by evil lusts and desires, with the result that they will be careless in the things of God for themselves, and will be despised and shunned by others as unfit.

The fact that on the subject of wives the Holy Spirit defines discipline and holiness in terms of each one being the husband of only one wife, i.e, that no-one should have more than one wife [25(H1)a] (since then at the commencement of the church there were those who came to Christ, both Jews and Gentiles, who perhaps had more than one wife) indicates and proves that the Holy Spirit does not frown upon the marriage of ministers, but officially recognizes that elders may live in the state of marriage without blame or guilt. For in both places, writing to Timothy and to Titus, where he writes: *above reproach, blameless,* the apostle goes on immediately to add: *the husband of one wife* [1 Tim. 3:2; Titus 1:6].

Marriage in itself promotes the work of godliness, it does not hinder it.

For although marriage involves temporal concerns, troubles and affairs which might be a hindrance to the work of the ministry, it also has many advantages in enabling the minister not only to live a disciplined and blameless life, but also to be more free of temporal cares and affairs and to serve the Lord more faithfully, zealously, and without hindrances; and especially at this time when the faithful and industrious ministers of the church are [126] so few in number, since the ministers of antichrist are still in a position to squander the inheritance of Christ in large amounts.

According to God's ordinance the woman is a help to her husband in everything, not a hindrance.

God has created the woman to be a help to the man and that they might live godly lives together. Therefore, when marriage has been entered on and continued in the Lord, the wife does not separate her husband from the Lord. And when the wife is also zealous for the kingdom of God, her husband will please her more not by neglecting the work of God, but by carrying it out faithfully and well. In marriage of itself there is nothing unholy, nothing which is not ordained and blessed by God. Therefore of itself it will not in any way hinder holiness and well-doing, but [25(H1)b] rather promote it; always provided that the marriage is in the Lord, which is particularly appropriate and necessary in the case of ministers of the church.

This means that all those who abstain from marriage without being called to do so by the Lord are not thereby made more free of worldly affairs and attached more devotedly and freely to Christ the Lord, but rather sink even more into worldly affairs and are estranged from Christ the Lord; this is something which, sadly, we have seen only too grossly in the case of our so-called priests.

When marriage was the norm for the church's ministry it brought much blessing; since being banned it has brought great uncleanness and offence.

But this is how it must turn out, when people want to be wiser and more holy than the Holy Spirit; for nowhere in the whole of Scripture by one single word has he indicated that marriage is to be avoided by ministers of the church, stating rather that he desires marriage to have the same status with ministers as with all those whom he has not appointed to live outside the married state, of whom there are not many. And this is why the first and better churches have been greatly blessed as they have not excluded the marriage of ministers; and as soon as it was excluded, it led to such unholy offences in the churches as are sadly testified to by the situation today.

How the holy fathers came to shun marriage.

In time the dear fathers came to understand Paul's word, in which he praises chastity outside marriage so highly, in far too broad a sense, and [127] in a way to shun marriage itself, just as if of itself it hindered holiness, which cannot be the case: because it is a work and blessing of God, ordained in Paradise, [26(H2)a] so that sin could not render it impure of itself.

But the dear ancient fathers did not consider this sufficiently, allowing themselves to think that in marriage there was too much carnality, and that therefore it was inappropriate to the ministry of the church, or indeed to any really zealous Christian life. This is why they then praised virginity and widowhood so highly, while on the other hand showing such an aversion to marriage.

Misunderstanding of St Paul's words, 'husband of one wife'.

It is the result also of many of them understanding Paul's words *husband of one wife* as if the apostle's requirement was for someone who had only had one wife throughout his life. Thus this interpretation entered the law of the church and was also confirmed by the Christian emperors, so that no-one anywhere is allowed to enter the ministry of the church, however holy and skilful he may be, if he has been married for a second time or was not married the first time to a virgin.

But this interpretation cannot rightly be drawn in any way either from Paul's words or from his teaching. What he says is: *husband of one wife,* not, someone who during the whole of his life has only had one wife, and her a virgin. In the whole of his teaching you will not find one place from which you could conclude that he abhors marriage for the church's ministry for the second or third time, to virgins or widows (so long as they are godly and honourable women). Moreover St Chrysostom and other holy fathers have understood and expounded this word, *husband of one wife,* [26(H2)b] in the way we have expounded it, which is and remains the only true and natural understanding.

The appalling mischief of the papists in not shunning any shame or vice in ministers of the church, and yet not on any account wanting to allow marriage.

But this exaltation of the chastity of the unmarried and disparagement of that of the married, although it was too great in the case of the holy fathers, was perhaps seen too well in those same pious fathers; because they demonstrated earnestly and perfectly true chastity outside marriage. But since our papists defiantly throw out the teaching and example of these dear holy fathers, and do not want by any dispensation to come to the lenient position of the dear apostle, indeed of the Holy Spirit, giving dispensation in the matter of marriage to ministers of the church [128] and accepting as good fellow-priests those married to a pious wife, because by their lives of utter shamelessness they have sadly troubled the church so grievously and terribly for so many hundreds of years now, every Christian can easily see that this is nothing other than a defiant mocking and deriding of the Almighty and of all respectability. For apart from this there is no shame or vice which they abhor in ministers of the church, even those which should not be spoken of; things against which they have the commands of God and of the church so frequently and so severely expressed, but which commands they have for so long trampled underfoot. And it is only this human rule which they maintain so tenaciously that they will not give dispensation from it in return for either money or goods, whereas otherwise for money they would put Christ himself and everything else up for sale.

Five reasons why the papists hold so tenaciously to the ban on the marriage of ministers.

But the antichrist knows well that if he does not allow or permit holy matrimony to his servants, but otherwise allows them all sorts of mischief, there is less chance of people of honourable [27(H3)a] disposition mixing with his crowd, who might do him an injustice and press for a reformation. He also knows well that the vice of dishonesty drives out from people all sense and feeling of piety; this can sadly be seen only too well with his whole crowd; so that the ban on marriage assists him in that there is nothing so godless and blasphemous that he cannot best employ in it his servants, the priests and monks. And it also leads to the whole of the church's ministry and the whole of religion being all the more despised and abhorred on account of the shameful lives of the priests and monks; and all the people themselves become more and more loathsome and godless, which is inevitable when the church's ministry and discipline are so despised.

But the antichrist also enjoys the fact that through all this he can obstruct and revile the Lord's holy work of matrimonial love to so many people. Lastly, the ban on marriage also assists the antichrist in enabling him to maintain and increase the robbery of churches, to the destruction of all thoughtless souls, and thus he is able to place the generation of the violent even more under an obligation to him to afford protection to his godlessness and tyranny. May our dear Lord Jesus save his poor lambs from these wolves and spoilers of the church.

Now, let us return to our plan. It is the will of the Holy Spirit that [129] the ministers of the church should first possess those qualities, whereby they in themselves and in those who belong to them may be an example of all holiness and discipline. [27(H3)b] Secondly he also requires those qualities whereby they may be an example of well-doing towards their neighbours. Some of these qualities serve to stop people being prevented from doing good to their neighbours, others to increase joy and eagerness in so doing. Avarice and the pursuit of gain prevent kind assistance being given to one's neighbour; this is why the Holy Spirit wants as ministers those who are not avaricious or given to the pursuit of gain, as the first and second texts show. Also they are not to be taken up with the affairs of this life, as the third text teaches, because this takes away the will, inclination and constancy to do good to one's neighbour and instruct him for his good. Nor are they to be self-sufficient, selfish, inclined to anger, quarrelsome, argumentative, and self-opinionated, or indeed timid in the gospel fight and inclined to presumptuous questions. Rather it is the will of the Holy Spirit that those should be chosen for the ministry of the church who are completely free of such failings, as shown by the first, second, third and fifth texts.

The qualities which make a man joyful and happy for the church's ministry

Principal among the qualities which the Holy Spirit requires in order that a person may be joyful and happy in helping his neighbour in both bodily and spiritual need are the following: that he should be fair, just, holy, hospitable, kind, patient, and reasonable, as the first, second, and fourth texts indicate.

Finally, the Holy Spirit also declares several qualities which are particularly helpful to the ministers of the church in carrying out the work of discipline and everything involved in shepherding Christ's lambs in a more effective and beneficial way. These are: being patient with the wicked, kind and faithful, [28(H4)a] industrious in teaching, managing his household well, being well respected and not a novice. This is taught by the fourth text. Thus we see with what qualities the ministers of the church are especially to be adorned, and of what vices and failings they are to be free.

Those things which may be tolerated in other Christians, but not in the ministers of the church.

By saying this we do not mean that these qualities are not called for in all Christians, and these failings should not be abhorred by all; but it should be known that these qualities should characterize and be seen in ministers more than in others, and there should be absolutely no hint of these failings in them. [130] For the rest, we have to put up with there still in part being these failings in the church, although it is a sad thing and something to be fought against. For it is often to be found that some have too much pleasure in wine and other things of the flesh; some still have too much affection for money and gain; some are too prone to anger and quarrelling—but you cannot on this account drive these people out of the church, because these failings of theirs cause themselves sorrow, they accept discipline and desire to reform their ways; but because they are in such a weak state and the ministry of teaching and building up the church requires the greatest strength and perfection in all good things, such people should not be appointed to the office of bishop or elder, although they may freely remain as ordinary Christians. In just the same way you cannot place just anyone in the council and government of a town, although he would be quite acceptable among the ordinary citizens.

Now we can all see how this serious approach to the choice and ordination of the ministers of the church has sadly fallen into decay under the papists, [28(H4)b] despite the fact that the whole of church law as set out by the ancient councils, emperors and popes most emphatically insisted on such a serious approach. This is why we pray with all our hearts to our heavenly Father: *Hallowed be your name, your kingdom come* [Matt. 6:9f.], and there must really be nothing on earth of greater importance laid upon us than the question of how we are to deal with this corruption of the church speedily and effectively. And if we are not yet able to have ministers who have entirely reached that goal indicated by the Holy Spirit through the apostle and who fulfil in every way the standard he prescribes to us, then let us still have those who are striving with real seriousness and eagerness to draw closer to that goal and to fulfil that standard to a greater degree. Because when those who are supposed to lead the poor people to Christ do not themselves strive towards Christ with all their hearts, who can express the trouble and disaster which must come about?

It is the responsibility of the churches of Christ to depose the false and faithless ministers and replace them with those who are true and faithful.

But the churches have been bought by Christ our Lord with his precious blood, that they should be his holy and free kingdom; now all things are theirs and they alone are Christ's, which means that it is not in the power of any creature to stop them turning away completely from the antichrists who under the guise of the church's ministry have been so miserably destroying them, and providing themselves with suitable ministers. Indeed, when they fail to do this they make themselves partakers of the ungodly nature and sacrilege of the false ministers, as St Chrysostom along with other holy fathers points out with great seriousness [131] in his fourth and [29)11)a] seventh epistles and also in other places. But I am talking about churches, not particular individuals: the whole congregations of Christ, in which Christian rulers are also to be found, not peculiar sects. And because the churches, too, are always to act according to the Holy Spirit and therefore the best order, they will carry out this deposition of the so-called but unfit ministers and installation of proper and suitable ministers with the involvement of their Christian rulers and the agreement of all Christ's lambs.

So far in considering from what people the ministers should be chosen we have placed great emphasis on spirituality and the provision of divine gifts for the ministry. They must have the greatest respect and confidence of the whole congregation, be most thoroughly known for their godly activity, and be very skilful and zealous in doctrine, discipline, and everything that promotes salvation, as well as being in the highest measure adorned with all virtues.

The church's ministry requires many sorts of gifts, therefore it is necessary to have many sorts of people in it.

But because the Lord does not give all these gifts and skills just to one, two, or three, churches have always had a good number of elders, and these not all the same in what they do and what they are. Because although all elders are to be well thought of and trusted and outstandingly adorned with all virtues, this does not mean that they have to be all the same in what they do and what they are, or that they are all skilled and equipped with the same gifts or one sort of gift. This is why the ancient churches did not only ordain to this ministry those who were learned or eloquent, but [29(11)b] also other spiritual, sensible and zealous men. In each one was recognized what God had particularly bestowed on him for the building up of the church. Thus in one it was recognized that from his youth he had been brought up in the faith and in the scripture, as Paul recognized in the case of Timothy; in another, that he was eloquent and powerful in the defence of the faith, like Apollos. In another it was recognized that he was of a kind and lovely spirit, someone from whom discipline and chastisement would be willingly accepted. Thus in each one something in particular was recognized which would be of service in the care of souls.

For the same reason the churches have not taken their ministers all from the same type of person as far as outward things are concerned: because God has not [132] distributed his gifts in this way. He does not look upon the person: indeed, in order that it may be seen that all Christians, high and low alike, are nonetheless one in Christ, ministers of the church have been taken from people of high, middle or lower classes, as each was found to excel in the necessary gifts for the care of souls.

For the sake of their recognition and approval by the people, and because of their geniality and good manners, it is often appropriate that many ministers are those born and brought up with respectable, capable people and friends: this was true of the majority of the ancient holy bishops, such as Ambrose, Augustine, Chrysostom and others. When, however, those who possess these advantages and gifts do not have sufficient understanding of matters of the faith [30(12)a] for themselves, let alone to be powerful in teaching and instruction of others, it is better for the churches to take those who excel in these necessary gifts of Christian understanding and zeal, even though they may not be so attractive and lovely from an outward point of view. Thus even though someone should come who is *able to speak in the tongues of men and of angels and fathom all mysteries,* if he is not faithful and zealous in the affairs of the Lord, it is better to take those who may be lacking in eloquence and learning, but are genuinely concerned with the things of Christ.

It is for this reason that the ancient well-ordered and apostolic churches chose their elders from people of all classes and types, as is indeed customary in the community at large, on the basis of their common sense and experience, in order not only that the public peace might be better maintained in the community, but also that the public need might be dealt with more easily and liberally.

St Ambrose complains that the churches do not have their elders from all sorts of honourable and sensible people.

This is why St Ambrose complains that already in his time churches had begun to be supplied only from the learned, and not as previously from pious people of all sorts. Thus he writes concerning 1 Timothy 5, 'The synagogue and latterly the church had their elders, without whose advice nothing in the churches was done; I do not know by what oversight this practice fell into disuse, [133] whether through sloppiness or more through the arrogance of the doctors, the learned or the teachers.' Thus this holy bishop declares that it is indeed a fault when the church's ministry is provided only [30(12)b] by those who are learned or teachers, and not by other God-fearing and truly zealous Christians.

How harmful it is that the bishops have taken all power in the church to themselves.
God wishes to use many in caring for his church, so it must of necessity be an evil thing when this task is restricted to a few.

And so it is an even greater fault that afterwards the bishops have taken almost all power in the church to themselves alone. Indeed, they say that the best form of rule is that which is exercised by one person, as God's rule is; but they show themselves to be very different from God. The care of souls makes so many demands that even in a small congregation it cannot be properly exercised by just one or a few. It is true that, as Plato also writes, people find it easier to have one leader amongst those called to exercise spiritual rule, than to have many. But there is so much involved in the true care of souls that even those who are most skilled in this ministry, if they are alone or few in number, will not achieve very much; because all skill and ability comes from God, who desires to carry out this his work in his church by means of many and not by means of few. In this work of building he wishes to have and make use of many tools, so that he may raise many of his own to honour and hold them all the more firmly together, as we have already shown. Others he gives to be apostles and evangelists, &c. None of his members must be idle, and there must be the highest degree of unity and order among them, each one must depend on and be depended on by the other; thus everything must be one and in common, beginning and continuing by means of common activity.

But we only need to look at the example of Paul, when he wished to hand over to Satan the Corinthian who had so grievously troubled the church; certainly, the apostle [31(13)a] might well have arranged this work himself, with someone else in the church carrying it out on his behalf. This is because this work of giving a man over to Satan to be tormented in his body, so that his spirit might be saved, is not something to be done by the ordinary church, but through the special personal gift of working miracles. But because the apostle was to carry out this work in the church at Corinth for its own well-being, he wanted them all to come together so that they could carry it out with him and he with them together, 1 Corinthians 5 [:1-5].

But from Romans 12, 1 Corinthians 12 and Ephesians 4, the passages which we quoted as the third, fourth and fifth texts in our first chapter, we have [134] the right foundation in these matters. Because there it can be seen most clearly how the Lord desires to have a group of people involved in the ministry of the church and uses many and different sorts of people in it, who also come from all classes and are of all types. And this is the fundamental and essential reason why it is necessary to ordain many sensible and zealous men of God of all classes and types to the care of souls, if it is to be carried out correctly and well.

Summary of what kinds of people are appointed to the ministry of the church.

This concludes our study of what kinds of people are to be in the ministry of the church, both in terms of spiritual ability and also of their outward characteristics. The purpose and aim in all this is that people should choose those who are truly skilled and also zealous for the work of the Lord, and those who can be trusted and who have the confidence of the church. These two characteristics [31(13)b] are accompanied by the others, such as that such people should be adorned to the highest degree with all virtues. Likewise that there should be a good number of them, because the Lord desires to carry out his work through them by means of many, not of few. And that they are to be chosen from people of all classes and types; because the Lord desires to bring those of all classes and types to positions of honour and to use them in this his ministry.

The Choosing and Appointment of Ministers

The apostolic example of the choice and appointing of the church's ministry.

Now, how these elders and ministers of the church are to be chosen and appointed is taught by the eighth and ninth texts. There we see how Timothy was given the gift of the church which was well attested through a prophetic message, i.e. the previous announcement by the Holy Spirit, with the laying on of the hands of the elders in the presence of many witnesses. We also see how Paul and Barnabas were chosen and appointed for their office as apostles to the heathen. The guidance of the Holy Spirit came as the dear saints gave themselves to the service of God and fasted, i.e. attended to all the things of God in word and sacrament, prayed and gave themselves to contemplating and praising the goodness of God, meanwhile abstaining from bodily food and all carnal activities. From this we now need to learn [32(14)a] that four things are required for the correct choosing and appointment of the ministers of the church.

Four things necessary for the correct choosing and appointment of the church's ministers. Above all we must pray to God to give us faithful ministers.

The first is that the churches should faithfully call upon the Lord and pray to him, at all times but with especial earnestness when ministers are to be chosen and appointed, that he would send skilful, faithful and [135] powerful ministers into his harvest field [Matt. 9:38], and show the church which ones he has chosen—as the first church prayed when they wanted to choose another apostle in place of Judas, Acts 1 [:24f]. The ninth text shows this.

In choosing ministers there must be careful scrutiny of which people the Lord has granted to be skilful and zealous for such ministry.

The second is that the churches must be most careful to pay attention to the directing of the Holy Spirit, in order to see who those are who are gifted with the fitness and ability really to build up the church of Christ, irrespective of any other considerations of persons or circumstances. Because where the Lord has given to people the will and ability to help in the edification of his church, this is the general guidance of the Holy Spirit that these are the people who should be chosen for this ministry.

Concerning Paul and Barnabas, Timothy and others in the early church special guidance by the Holy Spirit was given, but this is not the case generally. In the case of Apollos, Aquila and Priscilla were content with the general guidance of the Holy Spirit in that they found him to be learned, eloquent and zealous in the things of Christ. And so we, too, do not have to expect miraculous signs, but must pay attention well to the general guidance of the Holy Spirit.

[32(14)b] This is why in the fourth *[third]* text it is written: *The things you have heard me say in the presence of many witnesses entrust to reliable men who will also be qualified to teach others* [2 Tim. 2:2]. Here the apostle instructs Timothy to be diligent in discerning and recognizing those whom the Lord has gifted to be reliable and suitable for this work. This diligence and knowledge he also requires of him as he warns him not to be hasty in laying hands on anyone, i.e. before the people have been well tested [1 Tim. 5:22a].

Thus, when he orders Titus to appoint elders in the towns and immediately describes to him what they are to be like, *one who is blameless, the husband of one wife &c.* [Titus 1:6] he similarly indicates that those who should choose and appoint the ministers of the church must themselves diligently discern and, according to the common sense which God has given to them, faithfully decide who those are who show the most signs of the Holy Spirit, i.e. those who are best gifted, fitted and skilled for this ministry.

All ministers of the church should first be well tested.

This is why the apostle states concerning deacons something which is also to be diligently observed in the case of all ministers: *They must first be tested; and then if there is nothing against them, let them serve* [1 Tim. 3:10]. It is also shown [136] by the fact that he does not wish a novice to be chosen, who is not yet sufficiently well known. In addition the ancients did not allow a bishop to be chosen from another church when there was a suitable person to be found in that church who could be appointed as bishop. Similarly, that no-one should be elected to the higher ministry of the church who had not previously been experienced [33(K1)a] and proved in all the other orders of ministry.

All this shows what great diligence the churches, after they have faithfully prayed to the Lord for his guidance, are to exercise, how seriously they are to inquire, investigate and find out about everything, so that they are not deceived by false appearances and may discern and discover the true guidance of the Holy Spirit as to those whom they are to call and appoint to this ministry.

How those who are chosen are to be investigated and confirmed according to the old ecclesiastical and imperial laws.

This is how the ancient churches ordered these things, as they were also confirmed and legally commanded by the emperor Justinian, *Con.* 6 & 123. When one was to be ordained and installed as bishop, i.e. senior carer of souls and pastor, he was to have read out to him in the presence of the whole congregation of God by those who were to ordain and install him all the holy rules, laws and ordinances of the church describing the holiness and fitness required for this ministry. Then he was to be asked in the presence of all the people whether he had been legitimately elected, not having sought to obtain his election by means of gifts, payments, or promises, and whether he believed and trusted that by the Lord's help he would be able to fulfil his office as was fitting.

This was in order that if there was something wrong or lacking in either the election or the person, it might the better be learnt and acknowledged; because it was not likely that anyone would be able to claim or deny something concerning himself in front of the whole congregation, when there were in that congregation those who knew differently about him.

Therefore the whole congregation was also asked if they acknowledged him to be someone who was honest and suitable for this ministry, and who had been legitimately elected.

[33(K1)b] And if there was anyone in the whole congregation who wished to declare some impediment in either the election or the person, no matter who he might be and however he might declare it, this had first to be most searchingly inquired into, investigated and confirmed. The elected candidate was not to be ordained to the holy ministry before he had been found blameless by dint of this confirmation and the consensus of the whole church.

So this is the second thing, that it is necessary in the election and appointment of ministers of the church [137] that diligent care and testing should take place, in order that legitimate ministers should be chosen and appointed.

Church leaders are to arrange and conduct the election of ministers, according to the godly consensus and will of the people.

Thirdly, we learn from the above texts what order is to be used in this election and appointment. In the first place it is necessary to have the consensus of the whole church, because ministers are not only to be blameless in the eyes of the Lord's people, but also well trusted and loved by them. In the second place however, because it is only possible to receive the necessary testimony as to the suitability of ministers from the whole church, particularly if it is a large one, by the agency of a few who are particularly knowledgable, the other elders and leaders are to conduct and direct the election and carry out the installation. This comes from the fact that St Paul commanded Timothy that he was not to be hasty in laying hands on anyone [1 Tim. 5:22a]; and Titus, that he was to appoint elders for the towns, moreover appointing those who were blameless [Titus 1:6] and adorned with such virtues that there was no doubt that the whole congregation would be glad to accept them wholeheartedly as bishops. But this does not mean, [34(K2)a] as many maintain, that St Paul commanded Timothy and Titus as the leaders to appoint as bishops on the basis of their own authority and will those whom they wanted, irrespective of the will and consensus of the congregation. Because in all the ecclesiastical statutes it is especially laid down that no one should be given to be bishop of any church against its will, *Dist. lxi. cap. Nullus, et per quinque capita sequentia.*

How St Augustine appointed his successor.

Ever since the commencement of the church the leaders of the local churches have directed the election of ministers, whether it was carried out by all the people or by a certain number of the people specially chosen for that purpose. Among the epistles of St Augustine we have the records of the election and appointment of Eradius, whom St Augustine chose and appointed to be his successor. In these records we read that dear Augustine observed the following order: one day he summoned together the ministers of the church and all the people into the church and announced to them that he would like during his life-time to help to appoint a future bishop, to avoid strife and division on that account arising after his death. And then he announced to the ministers of the church and all the people that it was his will, and he believed it was also God's will, that one of the elders named Eradius should succeed him as bishop. As soon as the ministers and people heard this, they called out twenty-three times: 'Thanks be to God, [138] praise be to Christ', then sixteen times: 'Christ, hear us, long live

[34(K2)b] Augustine'; and eight times: 'You are our father, you are our bishop.'

Now this Eradius was so well known to the people that St Augustine had no doubt that the people wanted him to be bishop just as much as Augustine himself did in announcing this before the people. But still he wanted the shout of the people in which they declared their will to be recorded by lawyers and then subscribed by the other ministers and the people: therefore the church amongst other things called out twenty times concerning Eradius: 'He is worthy, he is right.'

For because the elders and bishops are to be so fruitful in their ministry, and must have the confidence and approval of the people, the dear ancient fathers were diligent in maintaining and ordering that it should be maintained, that no-one was to be ordained to this ministry without the consensus of the other ministers, the people and the leadership, as we read in *Distinct. xxiv. cap. Nullus. C. Episcopus, Dist.* lxi. *Cap. Nullus, Dist.* lxiii from the 9th to 29th chapter.

The emperor Justinian, in the law referred to above, commanded that there should be an order maintained in election and testifies that such order was also stipulated in the old ecclesiastical laws; this order was carried out in the following way:

The old ecclesiastical ordinance confirms that bishops, i.e. pastors and carers of souls, are to be elected.

When a bishop is to be elected in a church, the ministers of that church and the civic leaders come together and make their choice from three persons, putting it down in writing; but first each one is to swear an oath on the holy gospel [35(K3)a] that he is not casting his vote in the light of a gift or promise, or on account of friendship or patronage or the constraint of others, but only because they know that those whom they are electing are of the orthodox common faith and of honourable character. And this oath of theirs has to be included in the election document. This ordinance is to be found also in *Dist.* xxiii. *Cap. Illud statuendum.*

What canons are.

What has happened for a long time now to this holy election to the ministry of the church we must indeed regret, though we cannot write much about it. First the so-called priests removed the election of ministers from the congregation to themselves; then it was restricted to the senior prelates and those who called themselves canons, i.e. regular ministers [139] of the church who more than others live according to the holy canons, i.e. rules, which nowadays no-one either knows or obeys less than they do. For many years now the result of all this has been election on the basis of carnal favour and advantage and, if what we have been told is right, skill in maintaining and furthering the position, property, liberty and power of the so-called priests; as to the true care of souls, it is known and considered by no-one, or at least so few that they are unable to achieve or carry out anything.

But the more this election of ministers of the church has been corrupted by these people, the more pious and God-fearing Christians must apply all diligence to seeing that elections of the higher and middle orders of ministers are revived, and that those should be elected who are suitable for this ministry, i.e. capable [35(K3)b] and zealous to build the kingdom of Christ, being as such recognized, approved and loved in the churches.

If the churches have this aim they will readily arrange and hold elections in such a way that they are carried out both with the greatest diligence and in a spirit of good order and love. They will commit the direction and conduct of the election to those with the greatest standing and ability among the people; at the same time obtaining and seeking beforehand the will and consensus of the whole people, so that everyone will have cause to love and respect those who are elected, and no-one will have any objection. Because when the ministers of Christian doctrine are not wanted and loved by the children of God, they will not really be able to produce much fruit, however much they may be otherwise greatly gifted and in themselves honest and zealous people. But at the same time it must always be seen what reasons anyone has for approving or disapproving of a candidate; and the disapproval is based on untruth or wrong doubts, it must be gently removed by those who are truly understanding and spiritual.

The correct way of ordaining and installing ministers of the church.

The fourth thing for us to learn from the above texts concerning the election and installation of ministers is the great seriousness and reverence which are to accompany the installation of those who have been elected. Paul and Barnabas were appointed to their office with the fasting and prayer of the whole church, as indicated by the ninth text. In the same way great seriousness and reverence accompanied the proceedings of the elders in [36(K4)a] appointing Timothy to his office [1 Tim. 4:14].

False witness in the ordination of priests.

This is why it was the custom and rule of the ancient churches [140] always to present the elected ministers to the whole congregation and ask if anyone knew of any impediment or lack in them; the words and the form of this are still used in the ordination of priests. The ordaining bishop asks: 'Are they worthy?' and someone else answers: 'They are worthy.' Then the bishop again: 'Are they right?' and the other: 'They are right.' But sadly you can see only too well from the one who does the ordaining, his assistants and those who are ordained how inadequate a consideration and investigation this is to ensure the ordination of worthy and right ministers.

When, having been presented in this way, those who have been elected were judged acceptable, an earnest sermon was preached to them and to the whole church on the subject of the ministry, how those who were ordained to such a ministry were to behave towards the congregation and how the congregation was to behave towards them. This was followed by earnest prayer, an offering for the needy, and the Lord's Supper; and thus those who had been elected were ordained to their ministry with the laying on of hands as before and by the Lord himself, and comforted and assured of the Holy Spirit to enable them to exercise their ministry well.

This ceremony of the church finds its origin in the practice of the apostles, as the eighth and ninth texts clearly show; it was also faithfully observed as long as the churches were governed by true bishops, as we can read in the holy fathers.

Genuine apostolic seriousness in the installation and election of ministers of the church is everywhere still buried deeply from sight.

[36(K4)b] Now, sadly, the papists have made all this into a futile and idolatrous ceremony. Even in our churches, which are taking something of the reformation on themselves, the seriousness and zeal shown in the election and appointment of ministers is sadly still far from the seriousness and zeal of the apostles and the ancient churches. It is therefore not surprising that sadly so many and so great shortcomings are evident everywhere in the church's ministry. May the Lord grant to us that we should at last recognize all these shortcomings for what they are and make serious attempts to improve them. This is something which truly is of the greatest necessity if we do not want to get to the point where the Lord will take his kingdom away from us and give it to a people who will bring forth fruit.

6

What the Principal Work and Activity of Carers of Souls and Ministers Are to Be for the Flock of Christ in General and Individual Members in Particular

The ministers of the church are to provide for Christ's lambs everything the Lord has promised to them in his office of Shepherd.

Those who are ordained to the care of souls and pastoral ministry in the church are to serve our Lord Jesus, the chief Shepherd and Bishop of our souls, in his lambs, that is, all those elected to life, in such a way that through their ministry everything is shown and provided [37(L1)a] that our Lord has promised in his office of Shepherd. This involves being concerned and through the word of God providing that Christ's lambs, who are still straying from his flock and sheep-pen, should be gathered in; seeing that those who have been brought in should remain with the flock and in the sheep-pen, and when they do go astray again, leading them back again; and protecting those that stay with the flock against all temptations and afflictions, and helping them again if they fall prey to them; in other words, seeing that they are deprived of nothing which contributes to their continual growth and increase in godliness.

The five main tasks of the care of souls.

From this it is evident that there are five main tasks required in the pastoral office and true care of souls. First: to lead to Christ our Lord and into his communion those who are still estranged from him, whether through carnal excess or false worship. Secondly: to restore those who had once been brought to Christ and into his church but have been drawn away again through the affairs of the flesh or false doctrine. Thirdly: to assist in the true reformation of those who while remaining in the church of Christ have grievously fallen and sinned. Fourthly: to re-establish in true Christian strength and health those who, while persevering in the fellowship of Christ and not doing anything particularly or grossly wrong, have become somewhat feeble and sick in the Christian life. Fifthly: to protect from all offence and falling away and continually encourage in all good things those who stay with the flock and in Christ's sheep-pen without grievously sinning or becoming weak and sick in their Christian walk. [37(L1)b] These five tasks of the care of souls and pastoral office the Lord has beautifully summarized in the parable of the sheep pasture in Ezek. 34 [:16], when he says:

The number and identity of the tasks involved in the true care of souls.

> i. *I will search for the lost and bring back the strays. I will bind up the injured and strengthen the weak, and the sleek and the strong I will watch over and shepherd with justice.*

[142] *1. The identity of the lost sheep.*

The lost sheep are all those whom God has elected to his kingdom but do not yet recognize Christ our Lord and are entire strangers to his church, whether they were baptized into the church as children or not. This alienation from the flock of Christ and going astray in the case of many comes from their getting so deeply involved in the affairs of the flesh that they have no respect for

God and his kingdom; and when they are invited to the marriage-feast [Matt. 22:1-14] and the great supper of Christ [Luke 14:16-24], they say that they have other things to do: one has bought a field, another is trying out a new yoke of oxen, a third has taken a wife. In the case of many others they are hindered by false worship, as with the Jews, Turks, and the whole business of all the sects.

2. The identity of the stray sheep.

The stray and outcast sheep are those who [38(L2)a] have been with the flock of Christ and involved in the Christian life, but have gone away from it; but not yet to the extent that they have completely fallen away from Christ and been lost. Because those who do fall away eventually also come to the blasphemy against the Holy Spirit, that is, against the grace and power of God which they have recognized and tasted, having been offered and declared to them for their salvation. It is impossible to bring these back, as the sixth chapter [4-6] of Hebrews testifies. Indeed, they never belonged to us, the sheep of Christ, although they went out from us, 1 John 2 [:19].

But there are some who are led away, straying and outcasts from the flock of Christ, who nonetheless are truly Christ's and retain Christ in their hearts, although they may for a while entirely turn away and be estranged from the congregation of Christ and go completely astray, sometimes through involvement in carnal and worldly affairs, sometimes through false doctrine and false worship.

3. The identity of the injured and broken sheep.

The injured and broken sheep are all those who while remaining in the fellowship of Christ are hurt and injured in their inner being; it is as if they have destroyed and shattered a spiritual limb, i.e. the virtuous and godly ability to do those things which are excellent and right. For just as St Paul describes vices as our members upon earth, i.e. of the old Adam, Col. 3 [:5], so the skills, qualities and strengths which enable us to lead good and Christian lives are our members in heaven and belonging to the new Adam. These parts and limbs of the inner heavenly being are [38(2)b] injured, shattered, destroyed and broken through serious and gross failings and sins.

This includes all falling away or distancing oneself from the truth of Christ, as Peter fell away, and also the Galatians, in whom their faith, i.e. the head [143] of the inner man, was injured. In the same way it includes all gross injury done to one's neighbour, whereby damage is done to love, i.e. the heart and breast of the inner man: thus the Corinthians were damaged when they submitted one another to injustice and violence, went to law against one another before the heathen, and caused separation and schism among themselves. It also includes all gross immorality, whereby holiness and respectability, i.e. the blood and countenance of the heavenly Adam, become impure, ravaged and repulsive. This is also something which St Paul accuses many of the Corinthians of in 2 Cor. 12 [:21] and 13 [:2].

And just as all the virtues are like limbs and parts of the inner being, so when Christians transgress in thought, word or deed or fail in the matter of good thoughts, words or deeds, this always leads to these spiritual limbs being hurt or injured or broken. And although someone has perhaps been injured in only one limb, he still needs to be helped without delay, or it will lead to the corruption of the whole body.

4. The identity of the weak sheep.

The weak and feeble sheep are those who, although they remain in the church and do not fall into any of the grosser vices, and do not commit any notorious sin, are weak in faith and love and all the strengths of the Christian life. This includes those [39(L3)a] who are fainthearted in the face of bodily attacks; those who are slow and lethargic when it comes to helping their neighbours; those who are careless of discipline; those who err in right understanding. It also includes those who are afflicted by fevers, i.e. the disorderly stirrings of evil desires and lusts, their temperature ranging erratically between hot and cold due to anger, envy, jealousy, and addiction to fleshly lusts, with the result that they become diseased and weak in their Christian lives.

The sleek and strong sheep are the real Christians, who are growing well and are stable in the Christian life.

Now, the pastoral ministry in the church has to be so extensive, in order that all the lost sheep should be sought out and brought into Christ's sheep-pen, and that those who have once come to Christ and into his sheep-pen, but have become strays and outcasts again, should be restored; similarly, that the injured should be healed, the diseased and weak strengthened, and the sleek and strong well protected and rightly shepherded. [144] Therefore we want to bring before you and examine several texts in order concerning all these five tasks of the care of souls.

7

How the Lost Sheep Are to Be Sought

Luke 14 [:21b-23]

The ministers of Christ are to do everything they can to urge people into the fellowship of Christ, so that it will seem as if they are compelling people to come in.

i. *'Then the owner of the house became angry and ordered his servant, "Go out quickly into the streets [39(L.3)b] and alleys of the town and bring in the poor, the crippled, the blind and the lame." "Sir", the servant said, "what you ordered has been done, but there is still room." Then the master told his servant, "Go out to the roads and country lanes and make them come in, so that my house will be full."'*

John 10 [:16]

Note that the Lord will lead into his flock all who are sheep, and they will hear his voice. Therefore the Lord's voice must be proclaimed to all such lost sheep.

ii. *'I have other sheep that are not of this sheep pen. I must bring them also. They too will listen to my voice, and there shall be one flock and one shepherd.'*

Mark 16 [:15]

The gospel is to be preached in all the world and to every creature, i.e. to all people, whoever or of whatever sort they may be.

iii. *'Go into all the world and preach the good news to all creation.'*

1 Timothy 2 [:4]

Everyone must come to the knowledge of the truth, therefore the truth must be proclaimed to everyone.

iv. *[God] wants all men to be saved and to come to a knowledge of the truth.*

There are three things to learn from these texts. The first is that those who exercise Christ's ministry in his church are to seek to bring all people to the [40(L4)a] knowledge of Christ. The second is that they are to do this with the utmost diligence and unyielding persistence. The third is that the lost sheep are not won until they have entered Christ's sheep-pen, i.e. the full communion of the church, and have completely given themselves to Christ, their Shepherd.

All people are to acknowledge Christ as their Lord, therefore his kingdom must be proclaimed and offered to all nations.

The first point, that true carers of souls and faithful ministers of Christ are not to miss anyone anywhere out with the word of salvation, but diligently to endeavour to seek out all those to whom they may have access in order to lead them to Christ our Lord, is the testimony and teaching not only of the above texts, but also of all the prophecies and sermons concerning the kingdom of Christ which we have in the whole of Scripture. The Father has given authority to Christ our Lord over all flesh, he is to fulfil all things in heaven and on earth; every knee is to bow to him and every tongue honour and praise him. He is to rule until the end of the world, and all nations are to be his inheritance.

[145] Sadly however, not all are chosen by God and there are many who despise the salvation which the Lord offers them: this is shown in the parable quoted above, where none of those who had been invited would get a taste of the Lord's banquet. But it is not the Lord's will to reveal to us the secrets of his election; rather he commands us to go out into all the world and preach his gospel to every creature. He says: *into all the world* and *to every creature.* The fact that all people have been made by God and are God's creatures should therefore be reason enough for us to go to them, seeking with the utmost faithfulness to bring them to eternal life. [40(L4)b] That is why the Lord has expressed it in general terms: *to every creature.* He does not want to be invited to his banquet only those who show themselves to be citizens and inhabitants of his city, but he tells his servant: *Go out into the streets and alleys and bring in the poor, the crippled, the blind and the lame.* And again: *Go out to the roads and country lanes and make them come in.* From this the Lord teaches us that his ministers are simply to endeavour to lead to his church and to the perfect fellowship of his salvation all those who wish to come, no matter how wretched and corrupted they may be—indeed, not only to lead but to urge and compel them.

Those who are not sheep will reveal themselves when one seeks to drive them into Christ's pasture.

Those who are not the elect and do not belong to Christ's sheep will reveal themselves when, having been diligently sought, invited and urged to come to Christ, they despise the salvation offered to them and reject it, as the Jews did to whom the Lord says in John 10 [:26]: *But you do not believe because you are not my sheep.* So if anyone after being sufficiently sought and invited despises or even persecutes the kingdom of Christ, we have the Lord's command to shake the dust off our shoes and commit him to the Lord's judgment, not throwing salvation to the dogs or casting pearls to the pigs [Matt. 7:6].

With what unremitting and unyielding diligence the lost sheep are to be sought.

But the faithful ministers of Christ are not to give up lightly on anyone, as long as people are still people and [41(M1)a] God's creatures and have not shown themselves to be dogs by raging all the more against those who call them to the kingdom of heaven, the more faithfully such people want to assist them to find salvation; or in that the more attractively and gloriously the pearl of the holy gospel is presented to them, the more they despise it and trample it under foot. This is why the second point, the faithfulness, seriousness and diligence with which the Lord desires his lambs [146] to be sought, must be thoroughly taken to heart and faithfully considered. He desires that they should be sought wherever they are scattered, and sought with such seriousness and diligence that one should be ready to be all things to all men, as dear Paul was [1 Cor. 9:22], and even to hazard one's own life, as the Lord himself did, so that the lost lambs might be found and won.

How people are to be compelled into the kingdom of Christ.

And in doing this he desires that his ministers should be so far from being slack or negligent in bringing people to him that their earnestness and persistence can be likened to compulsion. *Compel them,* the Lord says, *to come in.* It is not that anyone can be compelled to come to Christ against his will, but that one should be so persistent with people that to the evil flesh it seems to be a compulsion and urgent pressing, because the Spirit in this way works against the flesh in order to lead people to Christ.

The lost sheep have not really been brought to Christ until they have committed themselves to the whole communion and discipline of the church.

The third thing to be learned from the above texts is the aim and purpose of seeking the lost lambs and leading them to Christ. This is, to bring them into Christ's sheep-pen so that they commit themselves entirely to Christ's care and pasture, listening to his voice in all things and also making use of all those [41(M1)b] things which the Lord has ordained to promote the salvation of his sheep. These things include doctrine, exhortation, warning, correction, discipline, comfort, both in general and in particular, through the word and the holy sacraments, holy assemblies, common prayer, thanksgiving, and caring for the poor. To sum up, Christ's salvation is to be experienced exclusively and entirely in the communion of Christ, as we have explained in the first chapter of this little book.

Therefore, since it is the Lord's will that his lost sheep should be led to his flock and his sheep-pen in such a way that there should be one sheep-pen and one flock, those who are to serve the Lord in seeking his lost lambs and bringing them to him are not to relax their service, diligence and labour for these lost lambs until they reach the point of wishing to be entirely in Christ's flock and sheep-pen; and to obey and follow in all things not their own understanding, but only the voice of their Shepherd, knowing that the shelter and pasture of eternal life indeed consists in what the Lord has for ever decreed and commanded for his people.

From this it may be concluded, first, that all Christians, as they are all members and instruments of Christ, and it is Christ, not themselves, who is to live in their whole lives (each according to his calling and [147] ability as Christ lives in each), are to serve the Lord above all and with the utmost diligence in order that all his lost sheep should be faithfully sought and led to him and brought into the fellowship of his church. Indeed, we pray for this before [42(M2)a] everything else: *Your kingdom come* [Matt. 6:10a].

How rulers are to assist in the finding of the lost sheep.

Secondly we conclude that, since those who are chief and great are appointed by the Lord to be chief shepherds of his lambs upon earth (because he wishes all souls to be subject to him), they are responsible to direct and employ all their power and ability as much as possible in order that the Lord's lambs which are still lost and wandering might be sought with all diligence and truly brought to him. These rulers are as God and Christ in the sight of and for all other people, and therefore they must also set forth and carry out in the sight of and for all others the work of God and Christ in continually seeking and saving that which is lost.

The rulers are not themselves to carry out the work of ministering the word and sacraments and exercising church discipline.

This does not mean that they themselves are to preach, or minister the word and sacraments and apply church discipline, because this is a special ministry and office in the church, as we have explained above; but since the rulers have the highest authority over all people and therefore more than anyone else are to see to it that everyone lives in a way which is right and proper and carries out his duties properly, this means that all rulers are more than anyone else responsible for seeing to it that there is no-one living among them who is not faithfully sought and encouraged to come to Christ. For quite simply, no-one can have happiness or salvation unless he is one of Christ's sheep and in his sheep pen. Here alone is to be found the shelter and pasture of eternal life.

Rulers are to provide the church with faithful ministers, see to the education and discipline of the young, and allow no-one to turn either himself or others from the sound doctrine and fellowship of Christ.

But rulers will see to this correctly when they follow the example of the ancient godly princes [42(M2)b] and rulers who ruled in a godly way over the people of Israel and the ancient pious Christians, in providing for the church's ministry and care of souls in such a way that the churches are not injured and harmed by wolves and hirelings, but have their faithful and industrious ministers who exercise the pastoral ministry and care of souls faithfully and correctly. Next, [148] they will see to the education and discipline of all the young people and encourage the teaching and fostering of godliness. Thirdly, they will not allow anyone to despise this ministry of salvation to old and young by either hindering others or turning away from it themselves, whether through false teaching or other folly or arrogance.

The imperial laws do not allow anyone to introduce or embrace false doctrine and sects.

We still have the laws of the old Christian emperors, in which they nowhere allow anyone to introduce false doctrine and separation from the communion of Christ, whether publicly in place of the ordinary church service or privately in corners and in the case of individuals. Nor is anyone who bears the name of Christ allowed to withdraw himself from the fellowship of the church and the holy sacraments: for those who do not remain with the fellowship of Christ are condemned as schismatics and barred from all honours and offices of honour. And those who embrace particular sects are encouraged to turn away from disaster by means of fines and other severe penalties: this statute and ordinance we still have in *Cod. De Sum. Tri. et f.c.l. Nullus* [43(M3)a] and in the whole codex entitled *De Hæreticis*, as well as in *Novellis, constitutione* xix.

St Augustine shows that they do not allow anyone who has been baptized to separate from the church.

How the people are to be compelled to be in the church.

And St Augustine praises and defends these imperial laws, describing them to the count and imperial chief Boniface, and also in other places, as Christian and beneficial; and proves from Scripture that kings and rulers only serve the Lord in their office when they forbid and punish with holy severity those things which are against God's commandment; and in the same way that they should take far greater care to see that souls should remain faithful to Christ their Spouse, than that wives should be faithful to their husbands; and that falling away from God should be punished much more severely than falling away in human affairs; and that those who have fallen away are to be urged and compelled to return to the Lord far more earnestly than a wife is to be urged and compelled to return to her husband, or a bonded man who has absconded to return to his master. And although a falling away which may be the result of ignorance is to punished more leniently, it is still not to be left unpunished. He also indicates how by means of this strict policy of the emperor very many wanderers were brought back to the church and true Christian communion. Therefore he identifies this urging and compelling from error to the truth, from sects to the communion [149] of Christ, as that compulsion of which the Lord has spoken in the previously mentioned parable of the great banquet in Luke 15*[14]*:[16ff.].

No-one can be compelled to any good thing against his will.

No-one should shy from this compulsion; for St Augustine is not teaching by this that anyone should be forced to believe against his will, which is [43(M3)b] the charge customarily laid against this doctrine. He knew full well that no-one can believe in Christ or do anything good against his will; nor did he want hypocrites who say with their lips that they believe, while with their hearts they do not. But the holy teacher saw that our kind God bestows his grace and success as much on orderly punishment and force to urge people to forsake evil lusts and desires and turn to sound doctrine and thus to conscientious well-doing, as he does on other words and works which he has ordained for the salvation of mankind.

God uses external punishments to bring trouble to people and make what is good attractive to them.

For as our merciful God and faithful Father, who uses both sour and sweet things for our good, often allows many people to commit great immorality and severe wrong and then instils in them a desire and love for discipline and right conduct, when through the appointed rulers they are steadfastly and severely punished for their immorality and wrong-doing, and forcibly restrained from their mischief; so the pious bishop and faithful carer of souls, St Augustine, discovered from the case of many thousands of people who were brought as a result of imperial punishment from the sect of the Donatists into the true communion of Christ, that our dear God uses punishment and prevention by force also to restore people from false doctrine and sects and contempt of religion. This he does first in order that they may hear sound doctrine and not be led astray or troubled by anyone else; and then through the doctrine he gives them his Holy Spirit, who rids them entirely of their errors, and makes them joyful and enthusiastic for the truth.

The punishment of those who are in error has its use even when they are not converted.

And when that does not happen and such [44(M4)a] people, so wrong in their love for themselves and their sinful contempt for Christ in others, remain in their error, one's responsibility towards them is fulfilled if one has tried the use of orderly punishment and force against them too, [150] and thus omitted nothing which

God has ordained to be done in such circumstances; and because he has commanded with such great earnestness that outward punishment and forceful prevention of all rejection and harming of religion should be carried out, this shows how very harmful and pernicious this wickedness is. For rulers are to be a terror to all evil works, and the more so the worse they are, Deut. 17 [:14ff.], Rom. 13 [:1ff.], 1 Tim. 1 [:8ff.].

In the second place, it is no small matter which one achieves in dealing with these people who are in error with such severity, if by punishment they are prevented from corrupting others as well as themselves; it is always more tolerable for someone to be wrong on his own account than for him to turn others into wrong ways as well.

Because people are born body and soul to belong to Christ and are committed to him in holy baptism, Christian leaders are not allowed to permit them to depart from the yoke and church of Christ.

It certainly does not mean, as not a few vainly imagine, that the appointed rulers should leave their people free to commit themselves to Christ or not; they have been given to Christ as his own by the heavenly Father, created and born for him, and they live and enjoy everything through him alone. If an appointed ruler is glad to compel by force natural people to remain with their natural masters, despite the fact that no-one can be faithful against his will and compulsion by itself cannot instil faithfulness in anyone, why should not one even more use force (which after all is all of Christ), as much as the Lord [44(M4)b] will grant, in order that they might remain with Christ and serve him? The fact that such force was misused by the antichrist for the purposes of godlessness does not mean that it is not in itself a good work and gift of God, which it is right to use for the purposes of the kingdom of Christ.

No-one should be pressed to make a false confession, or compelled to come to the Lord's table.

No-one is to be pressed to say that he believes what he does not believe, and still less to come to the Lord's table if he has no desire to do so, which is what the pope does. But also no-one who has been born and baptized into Christ among Christians is to be allowed not to hear the teaching of his Christ and to live publicly in opposition to it, blaspheming against it and making it odious to others.

Non-Christians are not to be admitted to any honour among Christians.

And since to Christians contempt for Christ is the gravest and most loathsome blasphemy, and they respect and honour godliness alone, it is certain that those who are real Christians will be able to have little delight in, and will not advance to any honour, any of those who despise the precious and blessed communion of Christ in the holy sacraments and all the activities of the church. But all those who absent themselves from these ordinances do in fact despise them; and they are announcing their intention to live as non-Christians by absenting themselves, since they are not allowed to absent themselves from the sacraments. [151] If they wish to live as Christians, then Christ has ordained this holy sacrament to be used by all Christians.

Among Christians it is only the best Christians who are to be appointed to government.

Since Christians should only appoint to government those people who are the most Christian of all, it is also fitting that they should not elect anyone to be a ruler who does not hold to the communion of the church in all things; [45(N1)a] as all the imperial laws command, in particular the nineteenth *Constit. in Novellis.*

So that if one of the non-Christians wanted to buy himself in falsely by means of the sacraments, one trusts that he would be known by his fruits to be a wolf in sheep's clothing. True fear of God and piety cannot be portrayed through empty appearances.

It is simply the case among Christians, as is sung in Psalm 15 [:4], that they *despise and shun vile men but honour those who fear the Lord.* Their government expresses what is sung in Psalm 101 [:6-8]: *My eyes will be on the faithful in the land, that they may dwell with me; he whose walk is blameless will minister to me. No-one who practises deceit will dwell in my house; no-one who speaks falsely will stand in my presence. Every morning I will put to silence all the wicked in the land; I will cut off every evildoer from the city of the Lord.* So let anyone play the hypocrite and put on an act as much as he can: this earnestness promotes godliness and drives away godlessness, if not from the heart, at least from the mouth and life, so that it cannot do harm to others. All this is taught clearly and thoroughly by St Augustine in the place we have referred to and many others; this is why I wanted to explain it briefly here, so that no-one should take exception to the fact that this most learned bishop, so wise in the things of God, identifies the use by rulers of punishment and the maintenance of religion by force as that evangelical compulsion into the kingdom of Christ, which Christ requires of his rulers and authorities.

How our rulers may also obtain for themselves a pious people.

[45(N1)b] Now let us return to our intended subject: when rulers are earnest in ensuring in such a way as we have described that amongst those who have been born to Christ the Lord and also committed to him in holy baptism, everyone should be properly sought, found and urged towards godliness, then our dear God will also surely entrust them with rightly seeking out and bringing to Christ those who by birth and breeding are estranged from Christ, such as Jews, Turks, and other heathen. This would be the case if they loved Christ's kingdom and desired to increase it in the same way that they love their earthly domains and are disposed to enlarge them.

[152] *Insofar as we seek the possessions and estates of unbelievers rather than to win them to Christ, God arranges that they should rob us of our possessions and estates.*

But sadly we see that people will seek to obtain the land and possessions of the Jews, Turks and other heathen, but regard it as of little importance that their souls should be won to Christ our Lord; and that is true not only of appointed princes, who are called worldly masters, but also of the so-called spiritual leaders.

They did not want to receive the Muscovites into the catholic church without payment of money.

Some years ago the Muscovites wanted to commit themselves to the communion of the catholic church, and they were only prevented from doing so by the pope insisting on them paying too much money. And because he could not receive the wool from these lambs, he wanted nothing more to do with the lambs themselves.

This is why God in his righteous judgment has arranged that, because we do not seek to win Jews, Turks and other heathen to the kingdom of Christ, but seek only to take away their temporal possessions and estates, [42(N2)a] they should rob us of our own temporal possessions and estates. Thus the Jews have sucked dry the poor Christians to a remarkable extent by means of their usury, and the Turks day by day strip us of land and people with violence, making quite alarming advances.

The severe wrath of God is also to be found in the discovery and conquest of new lands and islands, which people exult over so much, as if by this means Christendom was being greatly increased; in fact all that happens is that the poor people are deprived first of body and possessions, and then of soul through the false superstition which they are taught by the mendicant monks.

The people in the newly discovered lands are treated so inhumanely that they take their own lives.

The damage caused to our own people by the newly discovered islands and lands.

I have heard Jean Glapion, His Imperial Majesty's confessor, complain in front of important [153] people that the Spaniards in the newly discovered lands so forced and tortured the poor people to make them work to find gold and other things for them, that they could not bear the work and torture and took their own lives. Secondly, what is achieved as far as our own people are concerned? How many fine people are lost on the voyages, and when it is said that much has been achieved, all they can offer is the occasions and allurements of terrible wars, splendour and arrogance, and the oppression of the poor ordinary people; for through all this trade and conquest just a few get hold of all the world's goods and possessions and then use it to impose all sorts of mischief and power on the rest, many of whom can scarcely earn a dry crust by their hard and bitter labours. And then they call this the increase of Christendom. [46(N2)b] The Lord grant our princes and rulers the understanding and will to increase and improve Christendom in the right way.

Where Christians generally are failing in seeking out the lost lambs, this is to be undertaken by the ministers of the church.

Now, the elders of the church are always to see to the supply of those things which we have concluded in this article to be lacking in the seeking out of lost lambs by ordinary Christians and rulers. And if they do not have the apostolic call and command to go to foreign people, they must still see that in the churches where the Holy Spirit has appointed them as bishops and overseers no-one anywhere who does not belong to the fellowship of Christ is left to wander, but seek in every case to do what God always entrusts to them, in order to bring such people to the full communion of Christ.

Those lost lambs which have been baptized we must go after and seek out with the greatest earnestness.

And diligence in carrying out this task is principally due in the case of those who have been baptized in the name of Christ. For anyone anywhere to abandon these is to incur serious accusation by Christ our Lord; for in baptism these people were dedicated to and incorporated into Christ our Lord, to be brought up through the ministry of the church into the life of Christ and constantly encouraged in it. This means that those ministers of Christ who abandon the baptized (unless they have come to see that they are dogs or pigs, that is, such opponents or despisers of Christ, [154] that nothing can be done for them through God's word) will find it difficult to give account for them to God and Christ our Lord. Such disturbed and lost sheep may well, as God says through the prophet Ezekiel, [47(N3)a] perish in their own godless nature, but their blood the Lord will require at the hands of those whom he has appointed in his church to seek their salvation and to call them to repentance and the grace of Christ. Indeed, the Lord will accuse these unreliable and unfaithful shepherds with great dismay: *You have not searched for the lost* [Ezek. 34:4].

So may our only true and good Shepherd, Christ, grant that his churches everywhere may be provided and equipped with truly faithful and industrious elders who will not leave out anything so that all those to whom they have access and who belong to Christ, including Jews and Turks and all unbelievers, may be completely brought to him; and that these elders may exert themselves with special earnestness and godly enthusiasm for those who have been baptized but then led astray and corrupted, whether through so-called false religion or carnal luxury, with the result that they live completely estranged from Christ's sheep pen and pasture.

That concludes the consideration of the first task of the pastoral ministry and care of souls, that of seeking Christ's lost sheep and bringing them into the flock and sheep-pen of Christ.

8

How the Stray Sheep
Are to Be Restored

Luke 15 [:4-6]

Note that the faithful ministers of Christ must go after the one lamb which has gone astray and not give up until they have found it, and then they are to carry it back on their shoulders with all joy.

i. [47(N3)b] 'Suppose one of you has a hundred sheep and loses one of them. Does he not leave the ninety-nine in the open country and go after the lost sheep until he finds it? And when he finds it, he joyfully puts it on his shoulders and goes home. Then he calls his friends and neighbours together and says, "Rejoice with me; I have found my lost sheep."'

Galatians 4 [:19-20]

Such diligence, anxiety and distress is to characterize the work of restoring those who have gone astray that it may be likened to a painful childbirth.

ii. My dear children, for whom I am again in the pains of childbirth until Christ is formed in you, how I wish I could be with you now and change my tone.

2 Timothy 2:[24-26]

Note that all kindness and diligence must be employed in order to free people again from the devil's trap.

> iii. *And the Lord's servant must not quarrel; instead, he must be kind to everyone, able to teach, not resentful. Those who oppose him he must gently instruct, in the hope that God will grant them repentance leading them to a knowledge of the truth, and that they will come to their senses and escape from the trap of the devil, who has taken them captive to do his will.*

[155] *The identity of the stray sheep.*

We have already said which are the stray and outcast sheep, namely [48(N4)a] those who come out of the flock and sheep-pen of Christ and wander off, having once been with the flock and in the sheep-pen of Christ. This happens in the case of many through false doctrine and religion, as when the Galatians were turned away from the true faith and fellowship of Christ to the bondage of the law in the weak and miserable elements of the Mosaic ceremonies, and thus to the heresies of the false apostles. In the case of others it happens through love of this world, as St Paul complains in 2 Tim. 4 [:10] of Demas, who had deserted him and come to love the world again. This also happened to Mark, when he furtively left Paul and Barnabas, Acts 13 [:13].

Two kinds of apostasy.

These two examples of apostasy show themselves, however, as we have said, as being of two different types. This is because there are some who depart from the flock of Christ without completely falling away from our Lord Christ. Others, however, apostatize to such a degree that they alienate themselves entirely from the Lord; these go out from us, as St John writes in 1 John 2 [:19], but never really belonged to us, and have never committed themselves entirely to Christ. It is people like this of whom St Paul writes to the Philippians in chapter three [:18f.]: *As I have often told you before and now say again even with tears, many live as enemies of the cross of Christ. Their destiny is destruction, their god is their stomach, and their glory is their shame. Their mind is on earthly things.* So, too, were the lascivious widows of whom the apostle writes in 1 Timothy [48(N4)b] 5 [:11ff.]: *Some have in fact already turned away to follow Satan.*

All who have apostatized one should seek to bring in.

Now, since we cannot immediately know who have apostatized from the church of Christ to such an extent that they have completely and finally alienated themselves from Christ our Lord, we must apply the greatest diligence to bring back all those who have separated themselves from the church of God, whether this has happened through false teaching and so-called religion or through worldly and carnal excess, and leave no stone unturned until we have carried them too on our shoulders back to be with Christ's sheep and in the whole communion of Christ.

For what we said concerning the lost sheep applies equally to the strays. All those without exception whom we see separating themselves from the flock of Christ we must seek to bring in again, doing this with the most earnest and persistent diligence, and continuing to do so until [156] we have placed these sheep back in Christ's sheep-pen, that is, in the true and complete communion of Christ. This the above texts, as well as other Scriptures, all three clearly and expressly show and attest.

Meaning of the first text.
What it means to carry back the sheep on one's shoulders.

The first text teaches us that as soon as one sheep wanders from the flock, we are to leave the ninety-nine sheep and go after the one which is lost, and look for it until we find it. Then we are to put it on our shoulders and carry it back to the flock with the greatest longing and rejoicing; that means that we are to be, become [49(O1)a] and do everything for these stray sheep, and bear, avoid or suffer everything from them and for their sakes, until we have placed them back again in the true and complete communion of the church, to be pastured and sheltered by Christ in the church. If we are to do everything necessary in order to win for Christ all those who have never yet known him, as we have already shown, how much more are we to exercise all diligence, care and labour in order to lead back to him those who once acknowledged him and are still his and therefore specially entrusted to us?

Meaning of the second text, concerning the pain of childbirth.

Indeed, such diligence, earnestness and anxiety are to be employed to this end as to be likened to the pain and labour of childbirth. St Paul gives us his own example in this, as the second text declares. When a woman is in labour, what can she desire more, why does she undergo more severe pains and labour, if it is not to give birth to her child? Note therefore that this sort of earnestness, enthusiasm, anxiety, distress and labour are required in order that Christ might again be born and rightly formed in those who have fallen away, that is, that the stray sheep might be led and driven back into Christ's sheep-pen and the complete communion of Christ.

And this earnestness, enthusiasm and labour are required of all Christians and living members of Christ, but especially of the appointed chief shepherds, the rulers; and insofar as it involves the declaring and instruction of the truth of Christ, it is committed to the most distinguished of the ordained shepherds and carers of souls.

The rôle of rulers in helping to bring back the stray sheep.
And the rôle of carers of souls.

[49(O1)b] The rulers are to assist in this work by diligently driving out false doctrine and any incentive to do evil, and by earnestly encouraging people to accept Christian instruction from the carers of souls and to return to the fellowship of Christ. But the carers of souls themselves must go after these people with the utmost diligence, seeking in every way that God allows them, by means of clear and powerful identification and refutation of error and heartfelt presentation of the truth and redemption of Christ, to bring these people completely back from the [157] corruption and snare of Satan to Christ their Shepherd and his flock.

These must be those shepherds who leave everything else and undertake and do everything in order to bring back the lamb which has gone astray, not just by leading or driving it, but by placing it on their shoulders, as the first text which we have referred to teaches. They must be those mothers who give birth again with pain and distress, as the second text demonstrates. They must be the Lord's servants who will endure and bear everything, seeking and doing, with gentleness and keenness, in order to free from the devil's trap those whom Satan has taken captive to do his will: this is the meaning of the third text.

9

How the Hurt and Wounded Sheep Are to Be Bound Up and Healed

Matthew 18 [:15-17a]

Anyone who sins is to be corrected and put right, by his neighbour alone; but if this does not work, by the local church as well.

i. *'If your brother sins against you, go and show him his fault, just between the two of you. If he listens to you, you have won your brother over. But if he will not listen, take one or two others along, so that "every matter may be established by the testimony of two or three witnesses". If he refuses to listen to them, tell it to the church.'*

2 Corinthians 2 [:6-8]

Note that this person was punished on behalf of the whole church, and in this way was put right and had his wounds healed.

ii. *The punishment inflicted on him by the majority is sufficient for him. Now instead, you ought to forgive and comfort him, so that he will not be overwhelmed by excessive sorrow. I urge you, therefore, to reaffirm your love for him.*

2 Corinthians 12 [:20-21]

Paul wanted to heal the wounded Corinthians by means of severe punishment, and loved them so much that he considered castigating himself and bearing sorrow on their behalf.

> iii. *For I am afraid that when I come I may not find you as I want you to be, and you may not find me as you want me to be. I fear that there may be quarrelling, jealousy, outbursts of anger, factions, slander, gossip, arrogance and disorder. I am afraid that when I come again my God will humble me before you, and I will be grieved over many who have sinned earlier and have not repented of the impurity, sexual sin and debauchery in which they have indulged.* [50(O2)b]

Galatians 6 [:1-2]

Among Christians, each one considers the infirmities and sins of the other as his own, and does all he can to remove them and make them better, in all love and gentleness.

> iv. *Dear brothers, if someone is caught in a sin, you who are spiritual should restore him gently. But watch yourself, or you also may be tempted. Carry each other's burdens, and in this way you will fulfil the law of Christ.*

These texts teach us three things. The first is that the wounded sheep [158] are to be given treatment by all Christians, but particularly by the carers of souls; the second, that this treatment is to be given to all the sheep which are hurt or wounded; and the third, the nature of the treatment and medicine to be used in healing the wounded sheep.

We have explained above the identity of these hurt and wounded sheep: they are those who remain in the church and communion of Christ, but fall into open and notorious sins and abuses, such as abandoning their confession of Christ, denying the truth of Christ, and in other ways blaspheming against God, his holy word and all the things of God; disobedience and sin against superiors; any harm done to their neighbours' property, person or honour by word or by deed; all immorality and intemperance.

The wounded sheep are to be given treatment by all Christians, by rulers and by carers of souls.

So the first thing we have to learn here is who is to bind up [51(O3)a] and heal the hurt and wounded sheep. In the first place it is the responsibility of all Christians, for Christ must after all live and do his work in every Christian, but the ones who are principally to devote themselves to this work are those who have been specially appointed to provide care of souls and medicine for sins. The rulers are also to make their contribution to this, making provision both for special physicians of souls and for all Christians to fulfil their office in this respect faithfully and effectively; because it belongs to the office of rulers, to whom God has submitted every soul, that they should do all they can to see that all souls should live rightly and properly and in all things serve Christ our Lord, to whom the Father has given all authority in heaven and on earth, honestly and diligently.

All Christians are to help to bring sinners to repentance.

In the first text we see that the Lord speaks to every Christian: *If your brother sins against you.* Similarly in the fourth text the Holy Spirit commands that everyone who is spiritual, i.e. who is a Christian and desires to live a Christian life, is to help to restore anyone who is caught in a sin.

The work of punishment and reformation is to be carried out by carers of souls.

The second text, however, speaks of punishment by many and on behalf of the church; this punishment was called for by St Paul and carried out by the elders of the church at Corinth. Therefore we have set forth for us in this text the punishment and reformation which are to be carried out by the carers of souls. That the Lord requires such punishment is shown by his command that those who decline to reform after a private admonition are to be reported to the church, so that the church through its elders may also warn and punish such people. This is what [159] St [51(O3)b] Paul commands Timothy, when he writes to him: *Those who sin are to be rebuked publicly, so that the others may take warning,* 1 Timothy 5 [:20].

But in the third text we see even more explicitly how the ministers of the church more than anyone else are to be diligent and enthusiastic in applying medicine to hurt and wounded souls, and to supply what is lacking in what others do. This is why St Paul complained about the Corinthians, that he had heard that the church at Corinth had let someone go without being punished or making amends, saying that he wanted to grieve and humble himself, i.e. fast and pray, and thus make amends, in order that in this way he might arouse the whole church to appropriate zeal and solemnity in these matters. Indeed, he wanted to come himself to bring punishment and deal severely with those in respect of whom they had neglected their duty, as he writes immediately afterwards in chapter 13 [:1ff].

The healing of wounded sheep is a work of Christ himself, which he wishes to carry out through the agency of all Christians.

So we see first how those who are wounded are to be bound up and healed, by every Christian in respect of his neighbour, but particularly by those who are specially appointed to provide shelter and pasture for Christ's sheep. The main thing is this: this binding up and healing is a work of Christ which he has promised to carry out for his sheep, and therefore he does not want it to be neglected in any of his members; and he wishes it to be carried out with the greatest diligence in those of his members which he has particularly appointed to that rôle, those who are his under-shepherds, both rulers and carers of souls.

We should be concerned to give treatment to all sheep which are hurt.

The second point, that the responsibility of carrying out the work of binding up and healing all hurt and wounded sheep continues as long as they remain sheep and accept the voice [52(O4)a] of their Shepherd, Christ, is demonstrated by all the above texts and others too; for they are couched in general terms: *If anyone sins, If anyone is overtaken in a fault, If anything is hurt and wounded.* The Lord says, *If your brother sins against you,* and there is no need for any further reason for this help than that if he is a brother and has sinned, this help is to be rendered. Although the Lord says, *against you,* true Christians will let themselves be sinned against in every way they recognize that their Head and Lord Christ was sinned against and abused.

What the medicine accomplishes for those who are wounded.

The third point, the nature of the advice and medicine which we are to provide for the hurt and wounded, we learn from all the above four texts and others as well; for this medicine is nothing else than getting the one who has sinned to recognize his sin sufficiently to cause and move him to a position of true acknowledgment, regret and sorrow for his sin; and in this way [160] going on to comfort him again and strengthen his hope of grace, so that he may become enthusiastic and desirous of true reformation.

Sins must be pointed out so that they can be recognized and regretted.
How the sinner is to be won.

In the first text the Lord commands that one should point out and reveal the sin to the sinner in such a way that he is convinced of sin and overwhelmed by it, and thus be brought back through true repentance; he uses the word ἐλέγχειν, which means to point out wrong to someone clearly and convince him of it. And he goes on to say: *If he listens to you, you have won your brother over;* by using the words *your brother* and *win* he shows that he requires such punishment of those who have sinned [52(O4)b] as will be appropriate to and consistent with true brotherly love and a concern to win the brothers back from eternal death to eternal life. The sinner has not been won back until he has been moved and brought to the point of saying: 'I have sinned, I desire grace, I want to reform', and is really struck down and humiliated because of his sin; but also comforted again in Christ and has become entirely eager and passionate about putting everything right. Then the damage suffered by the hurt limb in his inner being has been truly bound up and healed.

The punishment of sinners is to be characterized by a gentle spirit and great love.

Therefore those who wish to correct and win sinners according to Christ's command will by definition do this with a gentle spirit, as required by the fourth text, and from truly heartfelt love which makes one willing and prepared to bear the sinner's burden—that love taught by the fourth text—and also to make amends for him, as with the example of Paul in the third text.

It is this sort of medicine that St Paul prepared and applied to the Corinthian who was referred to; he allowed him to be punished on behalf of the whole church, and also specially disciplined him himself in the power of his spirit, giving him over to Satan for the mortification of his flesh, in order that his spirit might be saved. In this way he brought this sinner to such regret and repentance for his sins that the sin in him was completely suppressed and killed. In order that this man should also then be comforted, brought to true reformation and strengthened in it, he wrote to the church at Corinth [53(P1)a] that the punishment and severity had been enough, and that now they should now rather forgive him, comfort him and show love to him, *so that he will not be overwhelmed by excessive sorrow*. And he forgave and comforted him as well.

How the Corinthian was healed.

From this it can be clearly seen what this spiritual medicine for injured and wounded sheep is, and how it is to [161] be applied. This Corinthian was severely injured in his inner being, his blood and skin had been vilely corrupted by dishonesty, but now the apostle together with the church at Corinth had purged him by means of correction and punishment, by this drastic treatment cleansing and removing the vile infection and the foul flesh. Then by forgiveness and comfort and the demonstration of love he had caused him to regain good healthy blood and clean and pure skin, and in this way healed him.

How Nathan healed David's injuries.

In the same way Nathan healed the injuries David had sustained through his adultery, manslaughter and grievous blasphemy of God's name, when he wickedly gave God's enemies victory over the people of God in order that Uriah might also perish. By sharply accusing him and convicting him of the great evil he had done, the prophet restored David's broken limbs and purged the foul matter of wickedness. This was truly accomplished in him when he said to Nathan: *I have sinned against the Lord*. And then the prophet comforted him again with the grace of God, saying: *The Lord has taken away your sin. You are not going to die*. Thus he truly strengthened him again and healed his spiritual limbs. [53(D1)b]

All spiritual health consists in faith in the forgiveness of sins.

Thus the health and life of the inner man consists in a true living faith in the mercifulness of God and a sure confidence in the forgiveness of sins which Christ the Lord has acquired and earned for us; because this faith and confidence make us truly love God and everything which pleases him, and bring us his good Spirit, who effects in us a right will and ability to avoid everything that is evil and to do everything that is good.

There are some sins which require drastic medicine.

But there are some injuries which require a long course of medication, drastic purging, cauterizing, cutting and burning, before they can be really healed, that is, with people being brought to complete remorse for their sins and entire purification of their evil desires and longings; it was an injury like that in the case of the Corinthian spoken of in the second text. This is why the kind and gentle apostle gave him over for so long to Satan so that his flesh might be mortified and his spirit saved. The punishment and ejection from the Christian fellowship of the church at Corinth brought great pain to him, too, because St Paul writes of him: *so that he will not be overwhelmed by excessive sorrow.* But this long and drastic medication brought great improvement both for him and for the others: in him it killed all the carnal wickedness, and the others it deterred from committing this or any other sin.

[162] *How David repented.*

It was the same with David's repentance, when he was afflicted not only with the death of the child which Bathsheba first bore to him, but also with the appalling and very severe punishment through the rebellion of his son Absalom. [54(P2)a]

The apostolic churches brought sinners to repentance of their sins by means of severe punishment.

The ancient and apostolic churches demonstrated the same severity against all serious misconduct, in order that they might move those who sinned to that godly sorrow which leads to repentance and which no-one regrets, and that in the congregation there might be maintained and increased that fear, as well as zeal and enthusiasm to live a Christian life, together with anger and hatred against vices, as testified by the holy apostle in 2 Cor. 7:[10f].

The origin of public penance.

This is where we find the origin of the public confession and penance of which we read in Tertullian, Cyprian, Ambrose and all the ancient holy fathers. When any of the Christians had in some way fallen into serious and public sin, through which others were offended, they were not admitted to the fellowship of Christ's table until they had given the church a clear and satisfactory indication of their repentance and reformation, and had done enough to prove that they were truly sorry for their sins and had given themselves with all their hearts to reformation of their ways.

The nature of this public confession, penance and satisfaction.

This satisfaction and proof of repentance and reformation had to be carried out, by those who had sinned and offended the church, in the following way. First they had to confess and acknowledge in the church before all the people that they had sinned and misbehaved; then for a time determined by the elders of the church they had to grieve [163] and atone for their sins with weeping and lamenting, with much earnest praying and pleading, with fasting and staying awake and abstaining from all bodily enjoyment, and with generous almsgiving [54(P2)b] and all kinds of Christian observances. By what they wore, ate, drank, and all they did they had to show themselves to be lamenting and seeking the forgiveness of sins with completely broken hearts and crushed spirits, and intending with the highest degree of longing and earnestness the complete conversion and reformation of their lives.

When and how those sinners who were required to do penance were restored to the Christian fellowship and absolved of their sins.

And when they had thus demonstrated to the church for the requisite time their repentance and sorrow for their sins and a true and steadfast determination to reform their ways, and had done these things sufficiently, and also by their example deterred from evil and provoked to innocence those whom previously they had offended through their transgression and encouraged to sin; only when all this had been done, the elders pardoned them on behalf of the church, publicly reconciled them to Christ the Lord and his church, loosed them from the bands of God's wrath, forgave them their sins in the Lord's name, and then admitted and accepted them once again to the Lord's table and all the fellowship of the church. The ancient holy fathers held very strictly to this practice of discipline and penance for sins, as you can read in all their writings.

The misconduct of Emperor Theodosius, which led to him having to do public penance.

The most holy and pious emperor Theodosius let his anger run away with him (which he was particularly prone to do, as St Ambrose himself writes) and committed a terrible murder in Thessalonica because of an uprising in which several of his officials had been killed. He had summoned the citizens to the theatre as if he was going to show them a play, [55(P3)a] and then ordered the military to attack them and kill them; in this way they executed some seven thousand people, guilty and innocent alike.

How this emperor did penance and was absolved.

After doing this serious act the emperor came to Milan, intending to go into the church and to the Lord's table, like the other Christians. This St Ambrose forbade him to do, in the sight of everybody, and in the name of Jesus Christ bound him to do penance [164] and excommunicated him from the church of Christ until he should have done fitting penance for the terrible murder and serious offence he had committed. For eight months the emperor bore this ban with Christian patience; and when, first through his steward Rufinus and then in person, he came to St Ambrose in the greatest humility, begging him with tears for the pardon and reconciliation of the church, St Ambrose would not remove the ban until the emperor had publicly appeared in the church among the penitents, fallen upon his face on the ground, and there publicly confessed and lamented his sins before the congregation of Christ. He also agreed, as the penance imposed upon him by St Ambrose, to publish a decree throughout the empire, and this he immediately published; in this way his remorse and penance became known throughout the empire, and all who had been hurt by his precipitousness in punishing the uprising at Thessalonica were gladdened by his penance, and all those who had been offended were compensated; and from this decree they saw clearly that the emperor was heartily [55(P3)b] sorry for the too hasty and severe punishment he had imposed, and that he had truly given himself to reform his ways.

In this decree he put a stop to all inopportune speed and severity in imposing punishment, both by himself and by other princes, and insisted on time for all such severity to be tempered; and therefore he published this decree not only in his own name, but also attached to it the names of Gratian and Valentinian the younger, his co-regents in the imperial rule, whom their father, Valentinian the elder, had appointed to be in effect guardians and therefore co-regents in the imperial rule.

The decree which Theodosius published as his penance.

This is what this decree says: if the emperors order someone to be punished more severely than is usual, having regard to the nature of the crime, then those accused who have been sentenced to be punished shall not immediately be punished or have judgment executed against them. Instead the circumstances and details of their situation shall be considered for thirty days. During that time the accused shall be bound and in custody, watched over by diligent guards.

[165] This decree the pious emperor Theodosius published and enforced in such a way that it was accepted everywhere and valued so much that later emperor Justinian incorporated it in his book of imperial decrees and commands, as we have it in *C. de pœnis*, beginning at '*Si vindicari.*'

Note that when the true bishops governed the church, this was the seriousness with which action was taken in the church against those who had injured the church by public [56(P4)a] and heinous sins.

This penance is God's ordinance.

These holy and faithful bishops took this serious attitude for no other reason than that it was commanded and required by Christ, and not just a human ordinance. For St Paul did not only keep this ordinance with all seriousness himself as a command from the Lord, but also rebuked others if they neglected this ordinance. He writes to the Corinthians: *And you are proud! Shouldn't you rather have been filled with grief and have put out of your fellowship the man who did this?* [1 Cor. 5:2] Note that the local church at Corinth should have grieved and lamented over this man's misconduct and put him out from them. He does not say: 'If he does not want to abstain from the trouble he is causing', but 'the one who has sinned by doing this thing'.

The man who sinned so grossly and publicly at Corinth was so full of remorse that it was necessary to guard against his falling into despair, yet he had to do penance and be excluded from the church of God for more than a year and a day.

And when the Corinthians allowed the apostle's punishment to take effect with them and made up for what was previously lacking, the apostle writes to them: 'The punishment which has been inflicted on this man' (i.e. the penitent) 'by many is sufficient for him. Now instead, you ought to forgive and comfort him, *so that he will not be overwhelmed by excessive sorrow.'* Note that the apostle warns the Corinthians that they should forgive this penitent, and that the punishment which had been inflicted on him by many, that is by the whole church, as the apostle ordered in his first epistle, chapter 5 [:1ff.], was sufficient. And he appends the following reason: *so that he will not be overwhelmed by excessive sorrow.* This man had now become so sorrowful on account of his sins that there was concern [56(P4)b] that he might be overwhelmed by excessive sorrow and even driven to despair, so he must surely have committed himself to reforming his ways over a long period, accepted the church's punishment with the greatest humility, and therefore really listened to the church. But he had not yet been forgiven, and had to remain subject to punishment and penance for such a long time; for the holy apostle, after writing the first epistle to the Corinthians, had sent to them first Timothy and then Titus, and it was only after all that, and after he had travelled far afield, that he wrote this second epistle to the Corinthians and advised them to forgive this penitent, and he would also [166] forgive him. This period was more than a year, as we can also see from the ninth chapter of this epistle to the Corinthians.

From this we can see that the apostle regarded this excommunication and penance of those who had fallen into more serious sins, even though they had turned away from their sins and were sorry for them, as an ordinance and command of the Lord, and not to be neglected in any church: otherwise he would not have blamed the Corinthians so seriously and sharply for neglecting it. He would not have been so concerned about a human rule.

Those who have sinned and not yet made amends the apostle threatens with severe punishment.

We can also learn this from what we read in 2 Corinthians 13 [:2f.]: *I already gave you a warning when I was with you the second time. I now repeat it while absent. On my return I will not spare those who sinned earlier or any of the others, since* [57(Q4)a] *you are demanding proof that Christ is speaking through me. He is not weak in dealing with you, but is powerful among you.* And similarly [2 Cor. 13:10]: *This is why I write these things when I am absent, that when I come I may not have to be harsh in my use of authority—the authority the Lord gave me for building you up, not for tearing you down.*

From all this we see how the apostle threatens the Corinthians with a particularly harsh and severe punishment: *I will not spare,* he says, and *so that I may not have to be harsh.* And in order to show that this severity and harshness are not meant to be an evil thing, he invokes the power of Christ in threatening them: *Since you are demanding proof that Christ is speaking through me; he is not weak in dealing with you, but is powerful among you.* In this way the apostle clearly demonstrates that this punishment with which he is threatening those who have sinned is a serious matter and command of the Lord, not a human ordinance.

He also demonstrates this by what he writes in the twelfth chapter, quoted above in our third text: *Lest God will humble me before you, and I will be grieved over many who have sinned earlier* &c. This being humbled and grieved he also required of the Corinthians in the first epistle, chapter 5 [:2a]: *And you are proud!* he writes; *Shouldn't you rather have been filled with grief?*

The meaning of being humbled and grieved in 1 Corinthians 9 and 2 Corinthians 12.

Now, this being humbled and grieved involved earnestly fasting, praying, and lamenting for sins, as we can see from all [57(Q1)b] the places in Scripture [167] where the ancient Greek translators have rendered the words for being humbled and grieved into their language.

This can be seen in Exodus 33 [:4], when the people had to atone for their transgression with the golden calf; and similarly in

Leviticus 16 [:29], when God commands the annual atonement for the whole community. Also in Judges 21 [:2], when the people of Israel lamented and fasted after being defeated by the Benjamites; and 1 Samuel 7 [:6], when the people lamented their sins and did penance for their sins. Then there was the penance of king Ahab, when he did penance for the murder of Naboth, in 1 Kings 21 [:27]. And similarly the repentance of the Ninevites, and all those of whose repentance we read in the Bible, and those whom the dear prophets warn when they are calling for true sorrow, repentance and expiation of sins.

God requires of innocent carers of souls that they should do penance for those who have sinned; how much more, therefore, does he require this of those who have actually sinned?

Well, dear Christians, let us see what follows from all this, what conclusion we should draw. This being humbled and grieved of which the apostle writes is an earnest mortification of the flesh, a fasting, lamenting, praying and pleading because of sins. This humiliation is required by the apostle also from the whole church in which someone had grievously sinned. Indeed, he regards it as so essential that he recognizes himself, as a chief carer of souls, as being responsible before God to take this humiliation upon himself, since those who had sinned had not done so. *I am afraid,* he writes [2 Cor. 12:21a], *that when I come God will humble me and I will have to be grieved.* Note that he recognizes that this humiliation is inflicted on him by God, not man.

[58(Q2)a] So the dear apostle considered that God required from him such earnest humiliation in order to do penance for the sins of other people, and indeed that he should take it upon himself if those who had sinned failed to do so—and he was one to whom all transgression was a matter of heart-felt sorrow, and who did all that he could to prevent, avert and put right all the sins of men. Therefore we can see very clearly how the apostle recognizes this correction, punishment and penance for more serious sins to be nothing else than what is most earnestly required by God the Lord; this is why he requires that the whole church, and in particular the carers of souls, should take it upon themselves to do this when someone in the church has seriously sinned and transgressed.

[168] *Penance was commanded by God in the law.*

And how else could the holy apostle have recognized the need for this humiliation and penance? He was led to do so by the Holy Spirit, who also led the dear ancient saints; indeed, he was led by the Spirit of Christ, who maintains and fulfils in believers all those things which God had ordered and commanded his ancient people by means of the letter, but now does so on his own account and for all time in a better way, freely and without the compulsion of the letter, and with a greater enthusiasm. But in Exodus *[Leviticus]* chapters 4, 5 and 6 we read of how God ordered and commanded his people that if any of his people, of the priests and princes or indeed the people as a whole, sinned against his law either by doing what was forbidden or failing to do what was commanded, they should appear before him in his church and before [58(Q2)b] the priests and there confess their sins, seeking grace, bringing their offerings, and in this way receive reconciliation through the priests. And this certainly did not take place without earnest humiliation, lamenting and fasting, as we have noted in several places above. In these places, and indeed throughout the Scriptures when there is reference to atoning for sins, we read that reconciliation for sins had to be achieved with this humiliation, lamenting, fasting, praying and pleading.

Why the innocent had to do penance for the guilty.

The fact that the whole church, and in particular the elders, recognized their responsibility to do penance for and with those who had thus grievously sinned is shown by Moses, Joshua, Samuel, Jeremiah, Ezra, and other fine and striking examples. Believers are members one of another, and so their leaders are for their part to take on the rôle of the head, which in all the sufferings of the members sympathizes most of all and has the greatest concern for them to be made better. Believers share in joy and suffering. Each one bears the other's burdens, acknowledging his own guilt in the sin of others. That is why they do penance with and for one another; and the ones who chiefly do this are those are to fulfil the ministry of the head, the true carers of souls, like Moses, Joshua, Paul and those like them.

We read of Moses in Exodus 32 [:31f.], when he lamented, prayed and pleaded for the people, that he asked God [169] to blot him from the book of life, or else to pardon the people. See also [59(Q3)a] Leviticus *[Numbers]* 14; and similarly Joshua in chapter 7 [:6] of his book, when he lay together with the elders all day long before the Lord lamenting and pleading, because it was Achan alone who had sinned by taking the devoted things from the city of Jericho, but thereby the wrath of God had been aroused against the whole people. God allows the churches to make use of all their members, and therefore they must bear the sins and share in the punishment of all.

From all this we see how the almighty and merciful God also prescribed to his ancient people this medicine for sins, in the form of earnest and public humiliation, punishment and penance. And this was such a serious matter that he imposed it not only on those who had sinned, but also on the whole people, and particularly on the leaders, the shepherds and carers of souls. We also see from all this how the true Spirit of God always led true believers to accept this, and made them willing.

In the church everything which helps against sin must be most earnestly carried out; and this is why the practice of penance is to be most strictly observed.

Now in the church of Christ everything that is good, everything that is useful and edifying, everything that is a medicine against sin, is to be practised far more completely, earnestly and enthusiastically than it was among the ancients; because the church has also more completely received the grace and salvation of Christ, whose work it is to save his people from their sins. How otherwise would St Paul and all the other apostles and carers of souls have so earnestly prescribed as from God this medicine against sin, a medicine so strong and therefore so effective in its healing powers, applying it themselves and vigorously prompting and encouraging everyone to do so, even [59(Q3)b] though this ordinance is not spelt out expressly to us in the same way as it was to the ancients?

The outward practices of the church were ordained by the Lord only in summary form, and were completely and universally appointed only by the apostles.

It should be carefully noted with regard to this and all the outward practices of the church that our Lord Jesus has spelt out very little of all the outward things which we are to do; and those things he has laid down, he has allowed to be dealt with in just a few words. We only have his written command in respect of holy baptism, the Lord's supper and penance, and least of all concerning the last. Concerning baptism the only order or command we have spelled out is: *Make me disciples of all nations and baptize them &c* [Matt. 28:19]. Concerning the holy Supper, we are just told that when we hold it we are to do it in remembrance of him. Similarly concerning this present matter of penance all we have is that carers of souls are to forgive the sins of all those who are sorry and promise to mend their ways. And what they bind upon earth is to be bound in heaven, and what they loose upon earth is also to be loosed in heaven; those whose sins they retain, they are retained, and those whose [170] sins they forgive, they are forgiven. But the dear apostles, or rather the Holy Spirit in the apostles, has given further instructions in this and other ordinances of the church, as to what the work of Christ requires and how they may magnify, display and make acceptable the work of God.

In the case of holy baptism and when it should be administered to adults, the Holy Spirit [60(Q4)a] has ordained that such people should confess their sins, renounce the world and the devil, and by personal confession commit themselves to Christ and the church; because this is what the apostles also did when people were baptized, as we read in the Acts of the Apostles, and they certainly did this only under the inspiration of the Holy Spirit.

Similarly St Paul condemned and punished the misuse of the holy Supper and taught and commanded the right use and attitude towards it, both in his writing and in addition when he later came to them, as he promised when he wrote to them.

What the apostles ordered to be done in baptism, the Lord's supper and penance.

In the same way the apostles also ordered what is necessary for genuine penance. All that was spelt out was that what the church binds and what sins it retains, that shall be bound and those sins shall be retained; and what it looses and what sins it forgives, that shall be loosed and those sins shall be forgiven. But as to what sort of people the church should bind or loose, whose sins they should retain or forgive, what they should require of or impose upon such people, we have no written command from the Lord spelling out all this distinctly and expressly. But we do have the acts of the apostles and how they dealt with this by the Spirit of Christ, as we have shown from the writings of St Paul; and the other apostles will doubtless have acted in the same way, since the one Spirit of Christ was leading and guiding them all.

[60(Q4)b] The Lord commanded St Paul and the other apostles to feed his lambs, and to do so in the most faithful and best way. This was all the command they needed in order to do, organize and require everything that might serve for the salvation of the lambs. But [171] the fact that this punishment and penance of those who have fallen into the grosser sins, which we have been speaking about, would serve for the salvation of the lambs, is something which they had learned long ago from the law and the prophets and were already used to; and they were led to it by the Holy Spirit, who governs the church of Christ.

God brings about penance for grosser sins in all upright people.

Indeed, it is not only the people of God, both new and old, whom the Holy Spirit has taught that special correction and punishment applied possibly over a good period of time are highly useful and beneficial, and indeed essential, for those who have fallen into the grosser sins; he also teaches all people by the light of nature. The father disciplines his son, not speaking to him for a while, perhaps even driving him out and not allowing him in his sight, if he has sinned too grievously and wantonly despised his father, until he really repents and thoroughly demonstrates by all his actions and attitude his sorrow for his transgression, together with the will and intention to mend his ways; and also going out of his way to avoid everything of which his father may not approve, and to do those things which will please his father. And if the child has done all this and shown his repentance over a good period of time, perhaps even for a long time suffering much poverty and distress, and yet the father does not restore him to his [61(R1)a] love and favour, then he has to come in all humility and ask him, often also sending others to ask on his behalf, and earnestly promise and undertake to do whatever the father wants.

What the severity of penance achieves.

In the same way pious masters will treat their servants when they have grossly misbehaved. And in all properly ordered communities those who have in some respect grievously done wrong must do appropriate penance and provide satisfaction and evidence of their improvement. And no-one is immediately forgiven when he turns away from his transgression and says he is sorry; because this punishment, discipline and penance make the people really reluctant to do wrong, and the mischief is somewhat removed from their flesh, and also others are deterred from sinning.

Since therefore God ordained this discipline, punishment and penance to be useful and beneficial for people, carrying it out by the agency of all pious fathers, disciplinarians and rulers, and in his church there should be the best discipline and government in order that people might be drawn, led and encouraged from all that is wicked to all that is good, he commanded this discipline, punishment and penance also to his people of Israel, spelling it out for them. But for his new people it is set forth and commanded through the dear [172] apostles, indeed through his Holy Spirit, as we showed above from St Paul.

It is as a result of this command of God and order of the Holy Spirit that public confession and penance, which we have previously referred to, were so earnestly maintained by the ancient holy fathers.

[61(R1)b] And in the case where someone who had grievously sinned was received into the fellowship of Christ and reconciled to the church without having himself provided satisfaction to the church through doing penance, the ancient holy martyrs and fathers regarded this as nothing other than a sinful transgression of Christ's ordinance and a clear corruption both of the sinner and of the whole church. We read of this in St Cyprian and other fathers.

How the church binds.

The Lord has given to his church the keys of the kingdom of heaven and the authority to bind and to loose, to retain and to forgive sins. What is binding and retaining sins other than to bind and hold to penance for their sins those who have sinned and come before the church as sinners who have despised Christ's redemption and fallen under the wrath of God and eternal damnation, to drive them to seek grace and improvement with all their hearts, with humiliation and mortification of their proud and evil flesh?

And the church is also to loose and forgive sins, doing this on God's behalf and therefore going about it with great seriousness and truth, and cannot loose or forgive the sins of anyone except the one whom they can recognize, as far as they are able, to be one who is truly sorry for his sins and committed with all his heart to mending his ways. But this true sorrow and commitment to reformation following more serious and grosser sins is not proved by someone just turning away from the sin he has committed and saying, 'I am sorry, I won't do it again.'

[62(R2)a] If someone (and this is an example also given by St Ambrose) has only greatly annoyed a human prince and thus forfeited his right to life, or has defected from him or in some way been unfaithful to him or is otherwise guilty of gross misconduct, what humiliation, confession, request and pleading will this person resort to, personally and through his relatives, what will he commit himself and undertake to do, in order to demonstrate true sorrow for his misconduct and a steadfast will to mend his ways? He does not consider that it would be enough simply to abstain from his misdeed and say, 'I will never do it again.'

[173] Then what sort of confessing, lamenting, being humiliated, praying and pleading, committing and undertaking themselves, should be resorted to and practised by those who rightly acknowledge and regret their great and horrible sins with which they have so severely angered the Almighty, their heavenly Father, and our Lord Jesus Christ, their only Saviour, and so harmfully offended his church, that they deserve eternal death? There is no doubt that no such person would ever think that it was sufficient actually

to abstain from the sin and say, 'I am sorry'; but rather like the first Adam, like the children of Israel, and all among them who have rightly acknowledged and regretted their sins, like Peter and all those in the church of Christ who have truly repented, and in the same way as St Paul teaches the Corinthians, he would with great terror and fear, with earnest humiliation and mortification, with fasting, praying, weeping and pleading, with the greatest eagerness to become pleasing to God, by suffering, avoiding, accepting and [62(R2)b] bearing, do or refrain from doing everything according as thereby he might hope to please God.

For dear Peter, too, it was not enough that he stopped denying the Lord, and that he was sorry, but he could no longer stay in the place where he had fallen down, but *went outside and wept bitterly*, lamented and mourned over his so grievous sin, until the Lord himself comforted him; and certainly while he was weeping and lamenting he allowed himself little bodily pleasure. It was the same with the people of Israel, whenever they had in some way gravely angered the Lord. It was also the same with David, Ezekiel, Jeremiah, Daniel, Paul, and all who lamented and repented of the grievous sins either of themselves or of others. What did the tax-collector in the temple say? Not, 'Well now, Lord, I will behave better and turn away from sins', but *stood at a distance, would not even look up to heaven, but beat his breast and said, 'God, have mercy on me, a sinner'* [Luke 18:13]. It was the same with the sinful woman in Luke 7 [:36ff.]: she did not stop with turning away from her life of vice, but went beyond that by getting in to see the Lord when he was with the unmerciful Pharisees, weeping there in front of everyone and lamenting for her sins, until the Lord himself absolved her and told her to go in peace.

So we can simply say that when people have fallen into the more serious and gross [174] errors and sins and have come through to a true acknowledgement of their sins, and have a right spirit as children of God, there will always be this lamenting, weeping, praying, pleading, [63(R3)a] confessing and repenting; and this is indeed a powerful medicine which will totally purge, cauterize and burn out all desires to sin and evil inclinations to offend, both in those who have thus grievously sinned, and also in the others who through this penance are moved to recognize clearly the horror and harm of sin, to consider and to recoil from sins all the more earnestly.

An easygoing attitude to sin is rife because the practice of penance is not observed in the church.

And who can deny that it is because there is no correction, punishment or penance in the church for sins, however horrible they may be, that the young people and people in general have become so much more easygoing in their attitude to all offences? Shame and disgrace have no place, and the poor people run amok and become, as St Paul complains, completely unrepentant and give themselves over to immorality and all vanity, never satisfied with the acts of their malicious and corrupt nature.

Summary of the reasons why penance in the church is necessary.

Now at length we have sufficiently demonstrated that this correction and penance for sins we have been speaking of is a necessary, beneficial and effective medicine against sins, and the only right way to bind up and heal the worse injuries and wounds of Christ's sheep, and that the gracious God and merciful Father has himself ordained and commanded this correction and penance for this people. This practice was also earnestly required and exercised by his holy apostles; and maintained with great enthusiasm and earnestness in his holy church, as long as right order continued and the church was provided with true bishops and carers of souls. By his Holy Spirit he has always led his truly obedient children to do this, and continues to lead them.

[63(R3)b] Now since this is the case and could not be otherwise, and if in other matters the holy scripture of God is authoritative for us, what Christian could doubt that all those who are ordained to the pastoral office in the church, and are to be the principal physicians of souls and guardians, are responsible to reintroduce into the church and apply this medicine of temporal punishment and penance for sins, and in this way again produce and restore to their proper use [175] the keys of the kingdom of heaven; and once again to carry out the truly beneficial practice of binding through penance and loosing through reconciliation?

However, this public penance which is to be imposed on those who have sinned is, as we pointed out at the beginning of the argument, a medicine for those more serious wounds and injuries which require somewhat drastic purging, cauterizing and burning.

Less serious daily faults are to be dealt with by daily repentance.

There are lesser transgressions which are committed every day, such as an accidental neglect of the word, prayer, and the ordinances of the church, or idle talk, or having too much desire for or being, to not too gross a degree intemperate in the use of those things God has given for our enjoyment. Similarly, failure to help and serve one's neighbour, without much harm being done to him; or being somewhat angry and ill-disposed towards one's neighbour, and so on. In those who are justified these failings and transgressions may occur seven times, that is many times in the day, and the Lord will have them to be forgiven seventy times seven times, Matthew 17 *[18]* [:22]. Christians confess and repent of these sins and transgressions in all their prayers and godly exercises, whether on their own or in the divine assembly. And whenever the [64(R4)a] carers of souls encourage this general and daily confession, repentance and reformation by their faithful exhortation, they are healing the sheep of Christ of these daily, less serious injuries.

Sins which merit the doing of penance.

But sadly many also fall prey to the grosser hurts and injuries to the inner being, which are those hurts and wounds of which the holy apostle speaks in the third text: gross and persistent *quarrelling, jealousy, outbursts of anger, factions, slander, gossip, arrogance and disorder,* gross immorality, lecherousness, and the like. And above all the more serious and intentional insults to God both by neglecting or even slandering godly practices, and by evil swearing and cursing. Similarly, grosser forms of disobedience of and contempt for rulers and all superiors. When the sheep of Christ have been injured with hurts and wounds like this, and the carers and physicians of souls become aware of it, it is only in this text of Paul that we see what is to be prescribed to deal with these hurts and wounds. It is certain that the apostle wanted to deal with them, that is those who had fallen into sins like this, not only by encouraging them to repent by his exhortation and example, but also by using drastic measures to prompt and urge them to repent.

Therefore, when there are true shepherds and physicians of souls in the church and the [176] churches are well and properly ordered, they will never remain silent concerning these hurts and wounds to the inner being which they learn of in the sheep of Christ, letting them carry on without penance, but when gentleness does not move such people to repent, they will like St Paul no longer spare [64(R4)b] them, but will show the power of Christ and employ drastic measures to bring about the humiliation and mortification of the sinful flesh and require some significant proof of sorrow and intention to mend their ways. For such shepherds and carers of souls are true servants of Christ in the care of souls and the pastoral ministry, and are recognized as such by the churches; will not the Spirit of Christ therefore work and act in them as well as he worked and acted in St Paul, and as he also ordered and commanded his ancient and coarser people? We have already shown this.

The most serious errors.

But there are still more serious and pernicious injuries, such as deliberate denial of the faith, adoption of false worship, deliberate sinful blasphemy, conscious enticement through false doctrine, murder, adultery, false judgment, false witness and the like.

These injuries require an even greater seriousness and zeal in correction and penance; that is why St Paul complains that the Corinthians have not all lamented and done penance in the case of the Corinthian who had irregularly taken his stepmother to be with him (which was one of the most serious of such injuries). And he writes that he was afraid that when he came to them God would humble him to such penance, for those who had previously sinned and not done penance, because of the impurity and whoredom and immorality they had been involved in—and indeed they had been most grossly and sinfully involved therein.

In this case the true care of souls required such serious penance, that the dear apostle considered that God wished [65(S1)a] him also to do penance on behalf of and with those who had so grievously sinned, taking up till that time so little notice of the man's sin and letting it go unrepented. And this is why it came to pass in the churches, as long as they were correctly governed, that those who fell into sins of such seriousness and then turned away from them were disciplined with long and severe penance.

How penance is to be practised with moderation.

But as to how long and how strictly people are to do penance, whether it is those who have fallen into more serious and damaging injuries or even the most serious and most damaging of all: the penance is [177] always to be moderated so that it is a true and beneficial medicine against the sin, and does not make the injury worse.

Those who are weak must be helped to sorrow by means of gentle penance.

There are three ways in which penance can do harm: firstly, when the severity of the penance causes people to leave the church completely and reject its discipline altogether, when by more gentle penance they might be brought to proper regret and sorrow for their sins and true reformation: better weak penance and meagre reformation, than none at all.

How those who refuse to do penance are to be regarded.

But when there are people who fall into the grosser sins and do not want to submit to any discipline or penance, these will also have no regret for their sins, but despise Christ and his church to such an extent that surely no true minister of the church could declare them loosed from the bonds of their sins and admit them to the communion of Christ. The Lord has commanded that only [65(S1)b] those who are repentant and believe in his name are to be loosed from their sins; and those who will not hear or accept his word from the church are to be regarded as heathens and those who have apostatized from the church.

The second way in which this imposition of penance can do harm is when it is imposed without proper earnestness and a faithful appeal to the conscience: in such a way that people may well accept the outward discipline and carry it out, without a heartfelt repentance and amendment of life. This harmful practice took hold in the church when the dissolute bishops no longer looked for sorrow of the conscience and of true faith, but only for outward deeds and mortification of the flesh, and determined the penance entirely according to whether the transgressions were great or small in themselves, without regard to the situation of the penitent.

Books of Penance. Carena. *Indulgence.*

This is why they made their books of penance, in which they set out the particular penance to be imposed for every sin. Thus for malicious killing, perjury, or divorce, there was first a *carena*, that is, forty consecutive days fasting on bread and water, followed by fasting three days a week (Monday, Wednesday and Friday) for seven years, and many other abstinences and penances; for less serious sins, fasting for a shorter period and less strictly, and other things to be abstained from. After a time they gave up the fasting and replaced it with prayer, feeding of the poor, or money, which was given for the relief of prisoners or the servants of God, as the monks were then called, or the poor or else to be placed on the holy altar. This in turn led to indulgences, [178] which are nothing else than [66(S2)a] the removal by the church of the penance which has been imposed.

As the bishops became courtiers, the proper practice of penance and the whole episcopal ministry fell into decline.

And so one abuse after another arose and increased through the dissoluteness of the bishops; and at the time when they started prescribing for sins not only penance but also temporal punishments, they had already begun to find their place more at court than in the church and to take to themselves the responsibility for worldly government rather than the care of souls. This began when the Franks, Charlemagne and his successors, were reigning, around the eight-hundredth year following the birth of Christ and subsequently.

From that time on penance and other practices of the care of souls were increasingly turned on their heads, until as far as penance is concerned it came to the point where public penance was not imposed upon anyone except malicious killers, robbers and arsonists, heretics (but not all of them), and loose women who wanted to turn away from their dissolute lives. And then it turned out to be more of a vain ceremony than a medicine for souls. Then even this more or less disappeared, and all that was left of the practice of penance was the imposition on people in confession of various prayers, masses, pilgrimages, and perhaps fasting and almsgiving. There was little emphasis on true and faithful repentance, as was sadly evident in both father confessors and penitents.

This reversal and complete abolition of the beneficial practice of penance all started with the carers of souls placing more emphasis and insistence on the outward activities than on true faith and heartfelt repentance. [66(S2)b] These outward activities, however seriously they are taken, can be undertaken by anybody, whereas true repentance and amendment of life can only be undertaken by those who in true faith commit themselves entirely to Christ our Lord, with the result that in them there arises and flames up a genuinely burning love and longing to live according to God's will, a hatred for sins and a zeal to crucify and put to death all sinful lusts and desires. But sadly this faith, love and zeal are not to be found in many; this is why St Ambrose writes that it was easier to find those who had remained innocent [179] than those who, having fallen, had genuinely and appropriately done penance.

The wisdom of the ancient fathers in the imposition of penance.

This is why the dear ancient fathers, from the time of the apostles onwards, did not assess penance according to the sins alone, like the dissolute bishops later on, but took into account the people who had sinned and their particular situation; they considered and weighed up the individual's circumstances and strength of Christian life, and also the circumstances of the whole church, and then prescribed the period and level of penance in order that both those who had sinned and the whole church were helped thereby to become more hostile towards sins, more free of sinful lusts and desires, and more zealous in all godliness.

Humillima poenitentia, August. ad Macedonium Epist. *54*

This is also why the dear fathers never imposed or permitted the major penance, which they regarded as a new baptism and a complete return from sins to God, more than once in a person's life, to prevent this penance being, as Augustine writes to Macedonius, lowly regarded and becoming just an outward [67(S3)a] activity which neither brought about nor encouraged genuine renewal to godliness.

The proper use of penance.

And so the second problem with penance, and almost the most dangerous of all, is when it is misused and made into a hypocritical outward ceremony and not used in the right way as God has ordered and commanded his church to exercise it: that is, to introduce the person to a deeper, but believing contemplation of his evil and what it means in terms of serious offence to God's goodness and his own undoing, in order that he might become the more avid for the grace of God and the more hostile to sins, submit himself the more heartily and entirely to God, and love him more ardently, the more that he recognizes that he has been forgiven; and that he might crucify and put to death in himself all evil lusts and desires, and awaken and ignite all zeal for the will and pleasure of God, 2 Corinthians 7 [:10f.].

The third problem with penance is when it is made so severe that the penitents sink into too great sadness and despair, which was what dear Paul was concerned about with the Corinthian. [180] True repentance must result from faith in Christ, and therefore there must remain the hope of grace; although there should also be fear and trembling because the great and inexpressible mercy of God towards us has been so severely offended and abused. Penance is meant to subdue and cast down the impudence of the flesh and make sad and bitter all pleasure apart from God; but this in order that one should have a greater vision, recognition, hope and love of the goodness of God in Christ Jesus our Lord, not that one should despair.

Great wisdom and spiritual astuteness are essential if penance is to be applied appropriately.

[67(S3)b] Because so much danger attaches to penance, as it does to everything that is useful and necessary, great diligence and true spiritual wisdom and astuteness are necessary in order to impose and moderate penance in such a way that people are caused, moved, brought and encouraged to exercise genuine, childlike faith and amendment of life in accordance with true faith; and that no-one should either be driven completely away from the church, which is the first danger with penance, not taught to play the hypocrite by an outward show of penance, which is the second danger, nor plunge into despair, which is the third danger.

However much danger and abuse there may be in connection with the care of souls, it is still essential and must not be neglected by true Christians.

And this is why the utmost diligence and earnestness in providing the churches with really suitable elders, which we spoke of in previous chapters, are of the greatest necessity, as is daily prayer for those who fulfil this office, that they may provide care and medicine or the well-being of souls; for even though such danger attaches to this medicine for souls and the devil has brought it into grave and prolonged misuse through his false ministers of the church, nonetheless all true children of God will never hold their heavenly Father in such serious contempt as not to recognize as essential and beneficial and to want to restore this ordinance of penance, which he has given to them and commanded them so earnestly, and employed so earnestly in both his old and his new people through his Holy Spirit to the great spiritual good of his own.

But since the old enemy of the church has attacked this holy and blessed medicine for souls, the practice of penance, so long and so wildly, [64(S4)a] it is also possible to find goodhearted people with no desire to despise the Lord's ordinance, who are of the opinion that this ordinance could not be of value in our situation and therefore should not be practised in our churches. Let us briefly consider this objection.

The first objection: if the sinner is overwhelmed by his sins so that he has been pardoned for them, what further need is there of penance?

In the first place they say: God has declared through the prophet Ezekiel that when the godless man turns from his sins and does what is good, the transgression which he committed will not be remembered. This is what he commanded his people in Matthew 18 [:15] and Luke 17 [181] [:3f.]. If the sinner comes and says he is sorry for his sins, they should forgive him. What need is there, then, of a lot of correction and penance, after the sinner has forsaken his sins, repented and desired grace?

Penance is a medicine for present and future sins, not past ones.

Answer: there is no need for it in order to obtain the forgiveness of sins, because the sins have already been pardoned by the mercy of God, nor to atone for past sins, which is done only through the blood of Christ. But correction and penance are needed in order that sins should be better recognized and shunned, and the grace of Christ treasured the more preciously, and more diligence used in order that this grace may not be received in vain, and that precautions might be taken to prevent the person immediately falling into sin again.

If we had the practice of penance in our churches, there would be a greater aversion to sins.

Who is so lacking in understanding of the things of God and of human ways and follies as not to be able to recognize this? When grosser transgressions were subject to earnest penance, as the holy apostle teaches and as was the holy [68(S4)b] and blessed practice in all the ancient, properly-ordered churches, there was brought about in all the children of God a more earnest aversion and detestation of sins and a very different zeal for true Christian living from that which, sadly, we discern among ourselves now.

The penance of Adam and the whole human race.

As soon as Adam turned away from his sins and sought God's grace, he was forgiven and God no longer held his misdeed against him. But God still imposed on him and all his offspring death and so much misery and sorrow with a view to penance and improvement.

The penance of the Israelites, Moses and Aaron.

In the same way he pardoned the people of Israel when they acknowledged their misdeeds and sought his grace, but still always imposed severe penance on them; he led them around in the desert for forty years, until all those who had come out of Egypt had died, with the exception of Joshua and Caleb. Similarly Moses and Aaron were not allowed to enter the promised land, although God had forgiven them their sins.

The penance of Miriam, Moses' sister.

Miriam, Moses' sister, spoke against her brother Moses and his office, and the Lord tormented her with leprosy; she soon acknowledged her sin and asked for grace, and Moses asked the Lord on her behalf. But the Lord answered: *If her father had spat in her face, would she not have been in disgrace for seven days? Confine her outside the camp for seven days; after that she can* [182] *be brought back* [Nu. 12:14]. There is no doubt that the Lord forgave her as soon as she was truly overwhelmed by her sin, but he still wanted her to do penance for seven days. And he certainly wanted this for her own good and for that of all the people.

Quid satisfactio?

This is how the Lord treated David and others [69(T1)a] to whom we have referred above; in the same way the apostles and holy fathers, indeed the Holy Spirit in them, also treated those who sinned. Penance is not a satisfaction for past sins, but a medicine against present and future sins, because it is intended to purge and purify the remaining lusts and sinful desires and thus to protect against future transgressions. This is how the ancients describe penance and satisfaction: satisfaction is rooting out the causes of sin and closing the door to incentives to sin.

For this reason all true physicians of souls are above all to console clearly with the forgiveness of their sins those who have sinned and forsaken their sins and are seeking grace, when they truly trust in Christ and are sorry for their sins. But since the Lord has commanded his physicians of souls that they are also to bind and loose in the church, binding by means of penance and loosing from the bond of penance, and in this way to release those who repent and commit themselves to mend their ways; how could it be appropriate for them to treat the matter of seeing that those whom they are to release truly lament for their sins and have committed themselves to mending their ways with less earnestness than any conscientious official must employ in releasing from custody those whom he has confined at the behest of his earthly master?

It is as if those subject to a lord have sinned seriously against their lord and thereby put their lives in jeopardy, and the lord accedes to their request to forgive them on the basis of their assurance [69(T1)b] that they will mend their ways, but at the same time wishes them to demonstrate their repentance and mending of their ways as an good example to the other citizens by some form of penance, in order that others should be deterred from similar misconduct and disobedience. And then such a lord commands his official: 'All those who are sorry for their disobedience and wish to mend their ways you are to pardon and grant them their lives, but at the same time to inflict some punishment on them as an example to others, and so that it can be seen that they are truly sorry for their sin and misconduct.'

Would it not then be necessary for this official, if he wishes to be truly obedient [183] to his lord, in pardoning these people at his lord's behest, at the same time to impose on them some form of penance and diligently discern if they are truly bent on mending their ways? And yet all those who had wished to mend their ways would be pardoned as soon as the lord agreed to do so, and would be completely assured of that fact as soon as the official informed them of it. And they would still be heartily glad to do the penance imposed on them and in this way to compensate the others whom they had previously offended. And this is why one describes as correction punishment like this and all kinds of punishment, even execution.

Since, as has several times been pointed out, everything in the church tending to sorrow for and rejection of sin is to be maintained and practised most diligently, why should this correction, discipline and penance not be [70(T2)a] maintained and practised most earnestly in the church of Christ? And this even though all God's disfavour is removed and complete forgiveness of sins is granted to us as soon as we repent of sins and seek his grace in the faith of Christ? But in this and all other matters required by true Christian communion, misunderstanding and offence come entirely from the fact that, sadly, we do not know or consider sufficiently what communion Chrsitians are to have with one another, and how far the true care of souls and obedience to the gospel, that is to true faith in Christ, extend.

The second objection: it is not right to withhold Christ's comfort from those who repent.

The second objection is: although it may perhaps be right, as a warning to themselves and for the benefit of others, to subject for a while to some form of church discipline and penance those who have in some way fallen into serious sin and grossly offended the church of God, it does not make sense to exclude them from the holy Supper when they have repented of their sins. Because those who have truly repented of their sins should be comforted; and communion with the Lord in the holy Supper brings the special comfort that our sins have been paid for by Christ our Lord. Since no-one can truly make atonement except in Christ, there is all the more reason to encourage such people to the communion of Christ, not exclude them from it.

[184] *Those who have sinned and repent are to be comforted in such a way that they are encouraged to complete repentance.*

Answer: In this and all other matters concerning Christian discipline, we must work things out not according to our reason, but according to the word of God. It is true that those who really repent are to be [70(T2)b] comforted and encouraged to take part in the communion of Christ, not excluded from it. It is also true that in the holy Supper the communion of Christ is imparted together with great comfort; but it is also true that the comfort of Christ cannot be rightly and profitably imparted, unless first one acknowledges and senses the corruption of sin, and therefore has a broken heart and contrite spirit and is filled with godly distress and sorrow; and *this godly sorrow brings repentance that leads to salvation and leaves no regret,* as the holy apostle writes and also we have quoted above, 2 Corinthians 7 [:10].

This is why God our heavenly Father has also ordained, and we have already adequately demonstrated, that those who grossly sin need first to be humbled, corrected, subjected to penance, and thus filled with godly distress and sorrow; not in order that they should despair and abandon all hope of mercy, but so that they might nevertheless lament and mourn that they have accorded so little value to and despised in so ungodly a way the eternal kindness of God towards us and the salvation provided by his Son.

In those who have sinned, the more hope they have in Christ, the more earnestly they repent and the more gladly they commit themselves to penance.

This lamenting and mourning will show itself all the more earnestly insofar as a person has a more steadfast hope in the mercy of God and is more established in the salvation of Christ. Because the more a person hopes in the mercy of God and the salvation of Christ, and the more perfectly he lives in Christ our Lord, the more he will also exalt and treasure dearly the kindness of God and salvation of Christ, [71(T3)a] and be of a godly mind through the Spirit of Christ. From this it must also follow that he will all the more shun, lament and crucify, both in private and before all believers, the sins, the contempt of the kindness of God and the salvation of Christ, the communion with Satan, to which he has turned away in his sins from the communion of Christ.

Then like a son who has grievously offended his father and yet has truly turned back to the love and will of his father, and will be all the more humbled before his father and pious brothers, and lament and make amends for his sins all the more earnestly, the more he becomes aware of the forgiveness and kindness of his father and brothers, and in this way his sins will pierce him all the more sharply; so every truly repentant Christian will commit himself all the more heartily and gladly to all the church's correction and humiliation, the more he becomes aware of the mercy of God and the [185] true love of all the saints, and the more powerfully he is affected by the Spirit of Christ. Indeed, it would be no different from someone coming with the prodigal son to the house of his heavenly Father, that is, to the church, and the more kindly towards him the Father and all the household showed themselves to be, the more heartfelt would be his confession of sins and giving over of himself to all punishment and discipline, saying: *Father, I have sinned. I am no longer worthy to be called your son; make me like one of your hired servants* [Luke 15:18f.]. Such a person would heartily desire to experience the fellowship of the suffering of Christ in his own flesh, and would want to be become like Christ in his death, [71(T3)b] in order that sin might be put to death in him, and also he might be united with Christ in the resurrection from the dead, and thus in all thing be found in Christ, not having his own righteousness but the righteousness of God, Phil. 3 [:9-11].

Thus those who have sinned and repented are indeed to be comforted and encouraged to share in the communion of Christ, but in such a way that they are comforted in God and truly partakers of Christ out Lord. And this requires, as we also see in Christ our Lord, that humiliation and sadness for sin should precede complete pardon by the church and full communion with the saints. Indeed, that true comfort in God and the communion of Christ which whose who have turned away from grievous sin desire to share in are in turn imparted and worked out in self-humiliation and sadness, as we see in the cases of David, Peter, the Corinthian, and all those who are set before us as examples of true repentance. We see it also in the parable of the prodigal son, who before his father ran to him, fell on his neck, dressed him in costly clothes and arranged a celebration meal for him, had to suffer misery and hunger for a long time and humble himself before his father and submit himself to all discipline.

Now, since the holy Supper is the most glorious and joyful remembrance and communion of the Lord, in which there is given and imparted the highest pardon, complete peace and perfect communion with Christ and all his members, the Holy Spirit has ordained and [72(T4)a] always maintained in his churches that, although those who repent are always to be comforted with the grace of God and salvation of Christ and are to be encouraged to share in the communion of Christ, which alone brings true atonement for sin, yet they are to be excluded and kept away from the holy Supper until such time as they have demonstrated their repentance in true humility so that the church may [186] completely pardon them and forgive their sins. In the same way with the ancients penitents were not admitted to the greater thank-offerings until they had fulfilled their penance and purification, although in those offerings the communion of Christ and forgiveness of God were not so gloriously and actually imparted as they are in the holy Supper. This table is ordained for the disciples of Christ, who are, indeed, one body and one loaf in Christ; but those are not to be accepted who are bound to penance and have not yet been forgiven by the church. And it is not right for them to forgive someone as soon as he says, 'I repent of my sins', when there is nothing to indicate that repentance.

The bitterly weeping Peter, the woman whose sorrow for sin was such that she washed the Lord's feet with her tears, the prodigal son who had done penance in misery so long and so hard and come to his father with a completely broken heart and contrite spirit and openly confessed and lamented his sins: these the church should forgive without delay and not withhold from them the holy Supper of Christ, as she has example and command in her Lord and Spouse. [72(T4)b] But not all those who desire the grace of Christ by their words demonstrate their repentance in this way.

The conscientious official whom we previously used as an illustration may indeed, when his lord orders him to show favour to those who have committed and reconciled themselves to mend their ways, not immediately communicate the temporal grace of his lord to everyone who says: 'I will mend my ways.' How much less, then, is it appropriate for the faithful servants of Christ immediately to promise the eternal grace of Christ to everyone who just says: 'I repent of my sins, I want to amend my life', without in any way having yet proved to the church his repentance and desire for amendment. God's stewards and servants are to deal in the things of God with truth and all earnestness. For how long did the most kind and merciful apostle require the Corinthian to do penance? We have spoken of that above. How long did St Ambrose require it of emperor Theodosius?

The supper of Christ is the highest means of grace, and therefore it is not to be shared with anyone whose repentance has not yet been recognized.

And because in the holy Supper there is imparted the complete and highest forgiveness of sins and pardon of those who have sinned, and yet faithful ministers may not forgive the sins of any unless they have demonstrated to the church their repentance and desire to mend their ways with real seriousness and clear proofs, [187] St Ambrose writes in his book *On Penance* that those who wish to be immediately admitted to the Lord's table as soon as they turn away from their sins are more desirous of binding the elders than loosing themselves; because [73(V1)a] by such untimely admission and forgiveness those elders themselves grievously sin and share in the sins of others, by not rightly applying to them the God-ordained medicine of penance.

The grievous harm done by sharing the Lord's table with those whose sin is known and repentance unknown.

It is obvious that people are still weak in their knowledge of Christ and have not yet been sufficiently taught concerning the kingdom of Christ, if they think that the holy Supper should not be withheld from anyone who desires it, and are not concerned what people are admitted to the highest communion of Christ and heavenly peace. And so you sadly see how many poor people there are who often cause grave offence to the church of God; who perhaps live for a long time at enmity with their neighbours, or have sinned and injured many by gross discord and slander, calumny and other notorious wrongs against their neighbours, or who have fallen into wild sexual immorality, serious blasphemy and contempt of God, and yet come to the Lord's table without any penance or sign of repentance, without even acknowledging their sins which they have committed against the church; indeed, even sadly often without turning away from these offences and without being reconciled to their neighbours.

If dear Paul were to write to us, who still treat such matters so lightly, as he did to the Corinthians, how much more sharply would he accuse us of our puffed-up pride and neglect of our responsibility to heal poor wounded sheep, than he ever did the Corinthians? And the holy martyr Cyprian would declare us to be guilty of the body and blood of the Lord [73(V1)b] and call us butchers rather than shepherds of the sheep of Christ with far more severity than he ever blamed and accused his own people for being too quick to admit to pardon and to the Lord's table those who had yielded to persecution.

Indeed, as we have already partly indicated, the antichrist has removed all discipline and penance from the church now for several centuries. If we are to take up the evangelical reformation, we must [188] undertake to restore them, and not give or promise peace through the holy Supper or otherwise to people who, because of their lack of contrition, are not entitled to have peace. We must also not strengthen the hands of the ungodly, who paint walls with paint which does not last, and push the cushions and pillows of false protection under people's arms and heads; and thus bring upon us as well the unbearable anger and terrible wrath of God, which the Lord promises the false prophets in Ezekiel 13 [:18ff.].

From the fact that everyone is to examine himself before coming to the Lord's Supper, it does not follow that carers of souls are not to require and encourage such examination.

There is another objection which some put forward on this subject, from the fact that St Paul writes: *A man ought to examine him-*

self before he eats of the bread [1 Cor. 11:28]. They say that there people are being told that anyone who does not wish to examine himself must take the risk upon himself. But these people must also consider that from the fact that the apostle calls upon everyone to examine himself, it does not follow that therefore he does not want carers of souls and those who exercise the pastoral ministry to do or contribute anything towards this examination; [74(V2)a] or that when the people themselves do not examine themselves and grievously offend the church, the carers of souls should neglect that very thing which he himself so earnestly requires and commands in 1 Corinthians 5 [:11ff.], i.e. that those who will not repent should be excluded from the church until they commit themselves to true repentance and amendment and prove this to the church's satisfaction, as we have already pointed out.

This problem arises when we are lacking in knowledge or consideration of what the Christian church and communion of saints are supposed to be, and what the pastoral office, the care of souls, and Christian discipline are supposed to be and achieve in them. Satan will not leave anything undone to create and maintain ever-increasing division between sheep and shepherds, sick and physicians, teachers and pupils, so that if the word of the Lord has got to be heard it will not be properly understood, and people under the guise of Christian living will continue to live in the flesh, without fear, without discipline, without zeal.

The objection that punishment by rulers deals with the matter so that ecclesiastical punishment and discipline are no longer necessary.

The third objection is: Although it may well be good to impose on those who have grievously sinned and desire grace again a period of penance, and to exclude them from the holy Supper during the time of this penance, there is no need of this in those cities and communities which have Christian rulers, who punish the grosser vices and do not tolerate offences. And for the majority of people

punishment by the authorities achieves much more than any ecclesiastical punishment or discipline.

The rôle and purpose of civil government.

Those who put forward this objection do not sufficiently know
or [74(V2)b] consider how great a difference there is between the
government of rulers and the care of souls by the elders in the
Christian congregation. The rulers [189] have the highest temporal
authority over all souls, by which they are to arrange and provide by means of teaching, discipline, laws, and all sorts of incentives and punishments, that among those whom they govern all
should play their part so that the whole community and all those
who are in it and belong to it live decent and holy lives and do not
hinder or harm anyone else in doing so, whether from within or
from without; and that those living in or among the community
should not only not offend or harm one another, but that no-one
should through immoral or dissolute living render himself useless
to the community and unsuitable to serve others.

The rulers appoint particular people for each teaching rôle, always with some
authority to exercise discipline.

But since the rulers do not take upon themselves the teaching and
exercise of their citizens in writing, and all good arts and skills of
body and mind, but delegate this task to those who are by nature
particularly gifted, skilled and experienced in these things, and
give those who are to teach authority to uphold right teaching not
only with words, but also, if necessary, by means of discipline and
punishments; good rulers will also appoint in all cases and with the
greatest diligence particular people for the subject of religion, who
will teach the people godliness, through which alone everything
good comes and is obtained.

The teaching of religion also requires its discipline and punishment.

And since this teaching of godliness calls for fear and discipline much more than any other teaching, [75(V3)a] inasmuch as this teaching of religion is intended to raise people from their corrupt state and nature to godly living, indeed completely changing and renewing them, all wise, honest and godly rulers, even among the heathen, have always been glad to permit, indeed to command and provide, that ministers of holy religion and teachers of godly life, that is, of blessed and eternal life, should also be endowed with spiritual fear and authority to discipline and punish all those who might thereby be increased in godliness.

Therefore, when our dear God gave rulers, of whom we [190] have never had very many upon earth, who earnestly punished all those who by speech, action or inaction showed their constant opposition to godliness, common peace and usefulness, discipline and good manners; they also saw, as Plato teaches, to the faithful maintenance of the teaching and warning of punishment, and what is most essential of all, to the possession and faithful exercise by the elders in the church of fatherly discipline and correction through the word of Christ, and that the authority of the Holy Spirit was measured and applied according to the folly of each poor conscience, so that true repentance and steadfast improvement through faith in Christ our Lord might be awakened and achieved in the children of God when they sinned.

Punishment by rulers is also a medicine for the soul and conscience for mature Christians.
The chief Physician of souls, Christ, has along with the discipline of rulers also ordained spiritual discipline for his people.

Godly people will also accept the punishment of the civil rulers as coming from God and Christ our Lord, who alone has and exercises all authority and rule in heaven and on earth, and therefore allow such [75(V3)b] punishment to take effect on their own conscience, since according to the word of Paul they are subject to the authorities also for conscience' sake [Rom. 13:5], at the same time remembering the forgiveness which our heavenly Father has promised to all those who turn to him when they are punished and console themselves in his mercy in Christ. But this spirit of holy acceptance and use of punishment by rulers is not to be found in many, and if in the Christian church all injured sheep are to be bound up and healed, that is, brought to true believing repentance and amendment of life, this will only really be instigated through the gospel and the spiritual ministry of the church. Therefore it is essential that over and above the general discipline and punishment of the civil authority, even if this is truly Christian and also diligent and zealous in applying punishment, the churches of Christ should have their own discipline and punishment: a discipline and punishment which are shown to be in the name, in the person, and on behalf of Christ our Lord, with a clear and compelling reminder of God's severe judgment and the satisfaction of our Lord Jesus Christ for our sins; and also of the earnest and comforting command which he gave his church to bind and loose on earth, what was to be bound and loosed in heaven.

And the main reason for it is this: our Lord Jesus, the only King and Head of the church, has ordained this discipline and penance for his church, as we have already shown, and has nowhere said that this [191] work of his should be omitted when the rulers are Christians [76(V4)a] who faithfully carry out their office by punishing wrong. Rather, just as he ordained ecclesiastical discipline and correction for his ancient people alongside the discipline and correction of godly rulers, so he has also testified to us clearly and openly through his holy apostle Paul, indeed through his Holy Spirit, who laid such emphasis on this medicine for souls, during the time not only of the apostles but also of the martyrs and holy fathers, that it is his will that this ecclesiastical discipline and correction should be even more earnestly maintained and practised, in that he rightly requires of us that we should be more diligent and zealous in the healing of all injuries to the soul than the saints of the Old Testament had ever been, because he has revealed salvation from sins more perfectly to us than he did to these ancients. And so if the church carries out this discipline with proper earnestness, the Lord, the chief Physician of poor souls, will bless it with success and great and remarkable fruit.

From this we can see the difference between the discipline and correction exercised by rulers and that exercised by carers of souls. Even when the civil authority fulfils its office of warning against and punishing wrong with the greatest diligence, it is still necessary for the church to have its own discipline and correction, which are practised in the name of Christ and by his Holy Spirit in accordance with his command about the keys.

Therefore, where the churches of Christ are properly cared for and God's kingdom stands in all its order, rulers will be most diligent in seeing that they drive out and uproot from their people by means of laws, warnings, punishments, [76(V4b]] words, and other penalties with regard to possessions, honours, or persons, all sins and transgressions and in particular, those which affect our holy religion, and will not allow anyone anywhere, whoever he may be, to go unpunished. But alongside that they will also promote with all diligence ecclesiastical discipline and medicine for souls, which are to be exercised by the ministers of spiritual binding and loosing. It is not only that this ecclesiastical discipline is more exactly suited to the conscience, but also that it has as well as its own command, its own spiritual success and fruit, through the Spirit of our Lord Jesus Christ. These are the keys to the kingdom of heaven.

The fourth objection: it is impossible in practice to reintroduce church discipline at this time.

The fourth objection raised against church discipline and the correction of those who have sinned is that it is impossible. Although, they say, in itself it would be good for the churches to have their own discipline and correction [192] and exercise it in every respect as it was in the apostolic churches, imposing mortification of the flesh, exclusion from Christ's table, and everything that goes with it; yet people have been corrupted by the popish ministers of the church for such a long time, and in this way given up all discipline and obedience, that the concern would be that in desiring to reintroduce church discipline one would be more likely to drive the injured sheep away from the communion of Christ than to heal them, and in this way fall into the first wrong use of penance, which we spoke of above.

They go on to say: in our churches, where [77(X1)a] now everyone is baptized and is supposed to be a Christian, there is not the opportunity to practise discipline and penance that there was in the churches of the apostles and martyrs, when the congregations were small in number and those who wanted to be Christians were driven close together by persecution and were kept in humility and serenity. This is because no-one would profess the faith unless he was serious about it.

We desire no penance other than that which Christ has ordained, and that is always possible and expedient.

In answer to the first of these objections, that for our people who are so corrupted and disobedient, church discipline would be neither possible nor expedient, but would be far more likely to drive people completely away from the church, our answer is as follows: we have no desire to reintroduce discipline or penance into the church except as the Lord has ordained them and commanded us to do so. Where there is the Lord's order and command, there will also be his Spirit and assistance, and with his assistance all things are possible and expedient. We have already shown that this penance and church discipline must be carried out with such spiritual wisdom and moderation that those who have sinned are not thereby driven away from the church, or caused to put on a hypocritical show of penance, or even cast into despair, but instead kept and built up in the church. Also, we are speaking here about that discipline we long for and which is to be restored with proper order in the fulness of time; we are not saying that we are suddenly going to turn to the actual practice of this ordinance of penance, together with that special order and occasion required by this work of Christ, and impose penance on people who do not yet know anything about Christian penance, or prescribe some [77(X1)b] drastic measure which people cannot yet recognize or use as a beneficial medicine against sins.

But anyone can easily see that when believers wanted to unite in the Lord and commit themselves to his rule, appointing suitable and well-intentioned ministers and acknowledging and considering them as the ministers and instruments of Christ; and these ministers desired to exercise their ministry in all faithfulness and with true Christian modesty, as we have already shown to be the teaching and command of Christ [193]—in such churches and congregations all the children of God would accept with heart-felt gratitude the blessed medicine for souls represented by all correction and penance at the hands of these faithful ministers and stewards of the Lord, or rather of the whole church and Christ our Lord himself, and in this way they would be greatly encouraged to true and blessed repentance and reformation and would be blessed, with none of them being driven out of the church. And when there were those who did not want to listen to the Lord and his church speaking in this ministry of the church, it would be the wish and desire of all the other members of Christ that these disobedient despisers of Christ our Lord and their own salvation should be excluded from the congregation, lest a little leaven should cause the whole of the dough to be leavened. Then there is no doubt that this church discipline would bring nothing but good and not harm, and would be possible and expedient, certainly not impossible or harmful.

That is all very well, those who still abhor church discipline [78(X2)a] will say; but we do not yet have any fellowships in the Lord like this, and the people are not yet ready to commit themselves to obedience to the gospel in this way. To this we reply: since this is the case, we have even greater responsibility to point out most diligently what it is that the Spirit of Christ requires of everybody, and also accomplishes in his own in order that we should call on him with all our hearts, that he should make us what we are not yet, provide us with what we still lack, give us what we do not yet have. And in order that we should not strive against Christ when he himself wishes out of his own great grace to help us with this medicine for our souls, which we have neither desired nor asked for, and that we should not say that we lack nothing and fall away, let us not think that we are already a properly ordered church and people of God just because we still have so much of proper Christian order.

We need to decide once and for all whether we really want to be Christians. If we want to be Christians and the Lord's lambs, we really need to listen to his voice, deny ourselves, and commit ourselves to him, so that he lives in us and we in him in such a way that at last we share together in that communion with him which is described above; we need to elect the sort of elders that the Lord requires, and then acknowledge, accept and apply the work of Christ in them as he has commanded us to do. If we do not pray for this with all earnestness and long for it with all our hearts, we are in no position to pride ourselves with being of true Christian [194] faith and spirit, and must ascribe the hindrances to Christian discipline and penance among us not [78(X2)b] to the time, or to popish corruption, or to preaching against the popish tyranny and about Christian freedom, but to our unbelief and false hypocrisy, as those who make much of our Christian faith and being but actually possess little, and have little desire to see everything arranged according to orthodoxy. And then we despise the word and command of the Lord, and consider it to be vain and harmful, despite the fact that he promises, offers and wishes to impart to us eternal life.

So much for the argument from the corruption of Christian people and the disobedience brought about by the papists, as a result of which it is claimed that Christian discipline would do more harm than good, and it would be impossible to carry it out.

Now let us answer the second of these arguments, from the fact that Christians are now so many and so mixed, claiming that there is not the same opportunity for church discipline that there was in the time of the apostles and martyrs, when churches were small and Christians few in number, and there were not so many non-Christians mixed in with them. Our answer to this objection is as follows: the Holy Spirit cannot be prevented from carrying out his work in his people, as he has done since the commencement of the church, either by the fact that Christians are many in number, or that there are many in all situations and ministries of the church who claim to be Christians but are not truly such. The Holy Spirit steadfastly and earnestly continued and carried out this his work of discipline and penance in his churches when they were far greater in terms of the number of people than [79(X3)a] they are now, and there were no fewer wicked goats among Christ's sheep or weak and sickly sheep than there are now.

Even in Paul's time the holy gospel had flourished throughout the whole world, as the apostle boasted in Colossians 1 [:6], and after that it continued to advance, and from the time of Constantine it became so dominant throughout the whole world that by the year of Christ 367 all the idol temples were closed and all idolatry and all heathen false worship were forbidden under the most severe penalties, and churches were established in every country, as far as the Roman empire extended at that time and even further than that; and [193] at that time the whole of Syria, Egypt, Asia, the whole of Illyrica, Greece, Italy, much of Germany, the whole of Gaul, Spain and Africa were still subject to the Roman empire.

In Milan St Ambrose probably had as many in his church as could be had in any of our churches, but he was able to maintain the practice of penance in his church, so that even emperor Theodosius had to subject himself to it, as we have recounted above.

St Chrysostom had his people, whom on one occasion in a sermon at Constantinople he estimated at a hundred thousand, and he also still retained discipline and penance, as did all the bishops at that time, although there was one who was both more zealous and more prudent in the encouragement of true reformation by means of penance.

Indeed, some may say at this point: this zeal did not belong to the church in general, but to these particular bishops. [79(X3)b] But anyone who has read church history and seen this custom described in the writings of the holy fathers knows that this church discipline was practised not only by some bishops who were of a more steadfast and earnest spirit, like Ambrose, Chrysostom, and others, but everywhere as a general discipline and medicine against the sins of the church. And this is also clearly demonstrated by the fact that this ordinance of penance and strictness continued until the advent of those dissolute bishops who wanted to replace it with laws, as we have previously pointed out.

Therefore we cannot find an excuse in the large number of people to enable us with a good conscience thus to neglect this ordinance and discipline of Christ, which is such a beneficial medicine for the Lord's wounded sheep. For no-one who reads the writings of the dear ancient holy fathers can deny that in their times the churches had more people than now, and yet they fruitfully maintained this practice of discipline and the ordinance of penance. If indeed Christ lives in us as he did in them, and we are moved by the same Spirit who moved them, we will long for this medicine for souls through penance with greater earnestness than is evident with us until now.

The weakness of Christians should be no hindrance to the practice of penance.

Just as we cannot find an excuse for our dilatoriness in this matter in the fact that we have a lot of people in our churches, neither can we find any excuse in the fact that among the Christians we have many weak and fragile people, or indeed many who are not Christians. Because in the [80(X4)a] churches of the apostles, martyrs, and holy fathers there were also many weak and fragile Christians, as well as many weeds among the corn and goats among the sheep, and yet they practised this medicine for souls [196] of penance and discipline faithfully and earnestly. What severe defects due to quarrels, divisions, arguments, factions and serious sexual immorality St Paul accused the Corinthians of in 1 Corinthians 1 [:10ff.], 4 [:6f.], 5 [:1ff.], 6 [:1ff.], 11 [:17ff.] and 2 Corinthians 12 [:20f.], 12 *[13]* [:2]. And what severe accusations the holy martyr Cyprian levelled against his people, as did Tertullian and all the ancients.

From this we can see that neither the large number of people, nor the fact that many of our people are sickly, can afford us an excuse not to make the most earnest effort to restore discipline and penance in the church, and indeed these very factors provide our greatest accusation and condemnation. Because the more numerous Christ's sheep are, and the more they are injured and wounded in themselves and also in great danger through the goats which are mixed in with them, by which they are daily even more injured and wounded, the more necessary it is that all Christians, all those in whom there lives our Lord Jesus, the good Shepherd who does not want his sheep to be left uncared for, and most especially those whom he has ordained to be physicians of souls, should be concerned and exert the greatest diligence and earnestness in order that this medicine for souls might be once again properly recognized, prescribed and accepted.

When those who are temporal rulers have many people to [80(X4)b] govern, whether in towns, courts, armies, or navies, they will be all the more concerned to organize the officers and instructors in each situation as the well-being of that community requires. The ancient people of God were very numerous, but each tribe, each clan, each household had its own rulers and officers, and there were special captains appointed over thousands, over hundreds, and over tens, so that everybody could be looked after and all the sheep properly cared for. If temporal necessity (or indeed often mere petulance, which it would seem in the majority of cases sadly lies behind the wars which our princes wage against each other) compels people to arrange and regulate things in such a way that, however many people are involved, everyone is looked after and everyone's bodily needs are cared for, should [197] we not be much more compelled by eternal necessity to live a Christian life and heal Christ's poor lambs?

True, it will be said, but where are you going to find so many skilled physicians of souls, even if in terms of sheer common sense this is all possible and simple, as well as being commanded by God? The answer is this: if at the present time we have many Christians, there will also be many people who will be suitable for this ministry of [81(Y1)a] medicine for souls, and whom the Lord will equip with his Spirit and enable, once we really call upon him to do this; but if we have fewer Christians, then we do not need so many physicians of souls either. In every town and community you will find those who will allow themselves to be employed in the temporal business of the community; should we not much more find among Christians those who will allow themselves to be employed to further the salvation of souls, if only the communion of Christ was once again properly known among us and we desired to commit ourselves to him? And there would not need to be such an enormous number of these people if the churches returned to their proper order once more.

Thus it is obvious that the large number of Christians in our churches does not hinder, but rather encourages the provision of timely care to all wounded sheep. Neither it is a disadvantage that they are afflicted with many and severe injuries. However fragile, hurt and wounded they may be, as long as they are still sheep and remain in Christ's sheep-pen, they will listen to his voice and are to be retained in obedience to the gospel.

Therefore, if only this medicine of souls were prescribed and applied with the moderation and diligence we have spoken of above, this would and could only result, since this is a work and command of Christ, in the bringing of great piety and reformation, rather than merely being harmful or impossible. Also we would not continue to have the situation that there are sadly many of those in our churches who profess the name of [81(Y1)b] Christ in vain. For those who had been called to penance because of their public and serious sins, and would not listen to the voice of Christ our Lord and Shepherd, [198] and would not accept appropriate and beneficial punishment of their sins in the church, would also not commit themselves to the communion of Christ, not yet being in Christ's sheep-pen.

This means that this medicine for the injured sheep could not yet be given to them, but first all diligence must be employed to bring them through the word of the Lord into his sheep-pen, that is, into full communion with him and true obedience to the gospel. We are speaking here of injured sheep which are already in Christ's sheep-pen and have submitted themselves to the word of Christ. At this point this must be carefully considered: in the case of someone who has not yet committed himself to the communion of Christ, there must first be carried out the previously described work of the care of souls; and the medicine of penance is not to be prescribed for such until they have entirely committed themselves to the communion of Christ and obedience to the gospel.

Let this be enough about the chief objections which are raised against the church's discipline and penance, so that we can at last conclude this article which we have spent so long on. But we have taken a long time over it because we are daily aware how few there still are who have a right understanding of Christian discipline and penance.

But there is still something which is a problem in this matter, and puts many people, even God-fearing ones, [82(Y2)a] off church discipline, and as the Lord grants us grace we must deal with this, too. It is that in their opinion it is out of this church discipline and penance that the popish violence and tyranny has grown up. Indeed, they say, it is because the priests persuaded kings and emperors and all rulers that they must be obedient and subject to them in all things, that they were easily able to exalt themselves to this position of power, pomp and tyranny over all rulers and authorities.

Our answer to this is as follows: in the first place, we do not teach that people should submit themselves to the priests or anyone else in everything, but only to Christ and his word. And when the rulers desire with all their hearts to live for him, they will soon recognize whether in discipline the elders of the church want to carry out the ministry of Christ or their own mischief. And when they discern error among them, they are not to be content with ignoring their intentions, but they are to punish them most severely; because all souls are to be subject to the ordained rulers who bear the sword, even for capital punishment: *They do not bear the sword for nothing* [Rom. 13:4]. In the second place, if our rulers were to ensure that elders were elected and regarded in the way we have described above as the Holy Spirit's ordinance, there would be little fear of violence or tyranny at their hands. This ordinance and work of the [199] Holy Spirit will, of course, not lead to anything evil or pernicious. In the third place, it does violence to church discipline and the ordinance of penance to say that the priests' violence and tyranny [82(Y2)b] grew out of them.

If you want to know the proper reason why the priests and the pope gained this great power, it is this. In the first place the great lords, and among them none earlier or to a greater degree than our own, the ancient Franks, reckoned that they could recompense God for their sins and wickedness by giving many possessions to the church and passing the power over these possessions on to the bishops, and then bringing these same bishops into the court, in breach of the public ecclesiastical law which we find strongly and earnestly set forth in the imperial statutes and regulations of the councils. Following that, when the bishops had become mighty barons and powerful at court, anyone who wanted to amass great possessions and extensive power would strive to obtain episcopal sees. And then it was not long before kings and emperors started bestowing these sees in return for money or favours, and for the benefit of members of their family, and in this way the sees became in time just worldly princedoms. This simony became rife first and most blatantly in the case of the Frankish kings, who appointed bishops to baronies before anyone else, and this is why St Gregory often accused them in his writings, which he wrote to them for this reason. He wrote to King Hildenbrecht, King Leuthern (otherwise known as Lotharius or Clotharius), King Dietrich, King Dietprecht and [83(Y3)a] Queen Brunhilda, and we still have these writings among the epistles of St Gregory, who became pope in the year 592, counting from the birth of Christ.

[200] *If we reckon emperor Henry I, known as the Fowler, as we properly should, he is actually the fourth of that name.*

When in time this simony of kings and emperors took such a blatant hold that they bestowed almost every prelatical office in return for money or favours, and the bishops, especially in the German states, had become the most powerful barons, these two interests came into conflict and undermined first the authority of the emperor, and then that of the other princes; and the real beginning of it was with emperor Henry IV.

How pope Gregory VII destroyed emperor Henry IV.

For when pope Gregory VII laid this most serious charge of public simony against the emperor and let it be understood, putting forward a fine array of evidence (which he did not otherwise seek), that there should be restored to the church her appointed right to choose bishops and prelates, and that pious leaders should be appointed who would punish and remedy this pernicious simony and all the vices of the priests, he managed by his honesty to obtain a consensus of opinion against the emperor; the others had been prompted and given the opportunity by the great power of a number of bishops and the notable antipathy of virtually all the priests to this emperor, on account of his evil-doing. The power of the German bishops in the empire was then much greater than it is now.

How the papal power grew.

Once this pope had succeeded in bringing such an able, valiant and mighty emperor to the point where he had to throw himself on his [83(Y3)b] mercy, the other popes followed the example of this pope and in this way increased their outward powers, which at that time were by no means slight, ever more, until they were able to set themselves up as lords over the whole world, having all kingdoms and powers at their disposal and pleasure as their own property, as vicars of Christ, into whose hand everything is given which Christ has upon earth; and with complete authority, which no-one on earth is to question. It was not only the desperate Boniface VIII who claimed this for himself, but also other popes. Alexander VI also began to exercise dominion over the Angles.

[201] Thus anyone who wants to look at history correctly and judge according to the truth will have to join us in acknowledging that the causes and origin of all the improper power and tyranny of the so-called priests are to be found not at all in church discipline and the ordinance of penance, but in these things.

The first and principal reason is the deserved wrath of God at all our sins, in that our parents and we have not truly loved the kingdom of Christ our Lord, and not trusted in him with all our hearts and exclusively, but have wanted to atone with him for our sins without penance or reformation, by means of the works of men and giving up what we have too much of, and to buy him off by giving him what is his own.

The second reason is that the Frankish kings and emperors, and after them also other princes, lords and people of substance gave the church so much land and so many people, and then handed power over completely to the bishops.

[84(Y4)a] The third is that the emperors, having made the bishops so powerful, brought them into the court and exalted them to be princes of the empire.

The fourth is that the emperors allowed themselves to be to the grossest degree involved in simony and themselves pursued it, so that it is horrible to read how in the case of emperor Henry IV it came to the point where all prelatical offices were sold; so that it was really no wonder that because of this one reason the imperial authority began to be reduced by the pope, and in addition this emperor had been brought up to be evil and mischievous by the archbishop of Bremen, and was enough of a burden in many ways.

If Christian discipline had been maintained, the so-called priests would never have become tyrants like this.

Certainly, if the emperors had guarded their office faithfully, rightly maintaining and exercising their authority over the ministers

of the church, and had entrusted the church's possessions to faithful and valued ministers so that the bishops were not encumbered
with them, and had not brought churchmen into the court, and
had faithfully commended church discipline both to the bishops
and to the whole people, then the bishops would have remained
subject to the authorities and would have been properly kept in
their ministry. Then they would have applied Christian correction
and reformation to the sins of the kings and mighty ones, as the
old bishops did; and when the princes went grievously astray, they
would have absolved them not in return for fields and meadows,
land and people, but only when they, like emperor [202] Theodosius,
had shown their true repentance and reformation. In this way both
offices would have remained free of their pitiful [84(Y4)b] confusion,
and the rulers would have maintained and encouraged the bishops
and carers of souls in their proper ministries, and in turn the carers
of souls and bishops would have done the same for the rulers.

How the emperors and kings made the bishops despise first God and then themselves.

But because the emperors themselves first gave the bishops lands
and people to rule over, and granted them complete authority over
these lands and people and all church possessions; and then, in
order that they might also enjoy the church possessions which had
now become much too great, and this not just for the benefit of
the empire but also for their own splendour, and often with no
good purposes, they made the bishops into princes of the empire
and employed them at court, on war business, and in a number of
very shrewd and dishonourable affairs; and they stood by while
they involved themselves in all sorts of ungodliness and open
simony and corruption of the church, and even assisted them and
colluded with them, in complete contradiction and breach of
their own ecclesiastical laws as set out in the *Codex* and *Novellæ*.
Therefore, on account of all our sins, the Lord also rejected these

emperors and kings, and because they had so abused their patronage towards the churches of Christ and Christ their Lord, and had deprived his churches of their ministers, giving these ministers cause, advice and assistance to become towards the Lord and the churches those who were disloyal and guilty of perjury and sacrilege, that is, thieves and robbers of God and murderers of souls—it is not I who have given them all these titles, but their own spiritual law and all the holy fathers many years previously— our dear God in his righteous judgment [85(Z1)a] has allowed these so-called priests also to become disloyal, perjured and rebellious towards the emperors, kings, and other princes and lords, and to appropriate to themselves and steal the imperial estates.

They have been able to release subjects from the vows and obligations they have undertaken to kings and emperors, and banish all those who kept their oaths and vows to their lords, and bring about terrible civil wars and devastation; and then to annex whole kingdoms and principalities, and steal from the empire the few prominent cities, in the German states, owned by the bishops in the [203] empire, which had not all been cities of the empire and imperial rule.

And so it is easy for any Christian who will consider how this severe deterioration caught on in the church to see that it was not that which gave cause for the tyranny, violence and pomp of the priests, but that the cause above all others is that church discipline had so completely fallen into decay among them, the ministers of the church and others; indeed, it is this and nothing else which has opened the door for the devil to all classes of people, to bring them into such apostasy and wrongness. With the kingdom of Christ's salvation everywhere disturbed, the tyranny of the antichrist has by this also been everywhere set up.

Therefore let anyone who is oppressed by the tyranny of the priests (as all Christians must be most grievously oppressed, since

Christians are to love and desire nothing more than the increase of Christ's kingdom) pray to the [85(Z1)b] Lord that church discipline might soon be restored to us, so that the church's possessions and power are not entrusted to anyone who does not truly serve in the kingdom of Christ; then the priests will all subject themselves entirely to the appointed authority, and leave the governing of lands and people to princes and lords and whomever else God calls, while they look after the churches; tithes and other ancient and proper church possessions will be employed by the agency of truly faithful and tested deacons for the blessed building up of the church, for the maintenance of widows and orphans and all those in need, for the release of prisoners from the Turks, and for all the general needs and necessities of men. And if anyone should fall short in some way, this discipline would lead him to mend his ways, or else the church would immediately dispense with his services.

Let Christian consideration be given to this by those dear lords who are always afraid when church discipline and order are mentioned that we want to diminish their authority, and the new priests want to be their masters as the old ones were. As the second chapter in this little book maintains concerning the kingdom of Christ, that everywhere in the church there is not to be hinted at or found any power or authority except that of our Lord Jesus Christ alone, this is the policy we will gladly follow, and give no opportunity for antichristian authority to priests or anyone else.

[204] Since the explanation of this article has been so long-drawn-out, I will now summarize it briefly, as follows.

All wounded sheep, i.e. those who are Christians [86(Z2)a] and are in Christ's sheep-pen and continue in obedience to the gospel, but fall into conscious sin, are to be given counsel and help so that through true repentance and amendment of life they may again become healthy and well, i.e. return to real, holy Christian life.

This counsel and help are to be shown by all Christians one to another, because Christ the Lord provides this counsel and help in all his people; but greater diligence is to be given to this by those whom the Lord has particularly appointed as shepherds and physicians of souls to his lambs, such as rulers, and those who administer the care of souls in the church.

And although the rulers are the chief shepherds, and the whole of their government should be directed to seeing that their subjects live Christian lives, and to that end are encouraged in all forms of service in the community as each one has his office and calling, because it is only by living the Christian life that we can live a life which is good and blessed; it is the carers of souls who have the special ministry of the word of Christ and the spiritual authority of the church, because they have been specially ordained to this and received the spiritual command of the heavenly keys.

But this medicine for souls, this counsel and help which are to be shown and given to sinners, the proper binding-up and healing of injured and wounded sheep, is in order that those who have thus sinned and yet remain in obedience to the church may be reminded of their sins in such a way that they may be moved and enabled to real believing repentance, and thus [86(Z2)b] to true reformation.

In the case of less serious sins it is the Lord's will that the carers of souls and special spiritual physicians of souls should heal them by the correction of the word alone. In the case of serious sins, however, alongside most diligent exhortation through the word there is also to be voluntary mortification of the flesh and temporary exclusion from his holy Supper, in order that those who have sinned should be led and impelled by means of such punishment and shame to deeper repentance and more earnest zeal to reform their lives. But in so doing moderation is to be used in order that no-one is frightened away from Christian discipline, nor cast into despair, nor tempted to make a vain show of penance by outward mortification.

[205] This is why this reminder must always take place through the word of Christ, with the consolation of pardon and all grace from our heavenly Father through Christ, although the seriousness of sins is also to be earnestly pointed out, in order that they may be rightly recognized and hated, and the grace of the Lord and pardon for sins be all the more preciously valued and ardently requested. For this reason drastic correction must often be employed, and that not with words alone, but also with bodily mortification and punishment.

And this is all because God ordained this for both his old and new people, and has always maintained and carried it out among them when they properly observed his ordinance, as is testified by the writings of the prophets, apostles, martyrs and holy fathers. It is only necessary to consider with proper Christian diligence the writings which we have previously referred to.

Why it is not enough for someone to say: 'I won't do it any more.'

[87(Z3)a] This, then, is the kernel of this chapter: may the Lord grant that it should it should be considered in a Christian way by all those who want to be Christians. And because nothing would rejoice Satan more than to cast misunderstanding and suspicion on all this truth and essential doctrine of Christ, there are two further things which I must maintain. The first I have set out several times: it is not enough reason to loose anyone completely from his sins and admit him to the holy Supper, that following the commission of grosser transgressions he has said: 'I am sorry, I won't do it any more.'

But note, pious reader, that I have also on several occasions added these words: if he shows no other signs of true repentance. The pious shepherd and physician is to make sure that poor sinners do not in this way attempt to deceive themselves and the church. The faithful father or conscientious mother will not be satisfied with a child saying: 'Nothing is wrong with me any more', without also making sure that this is truly the case.

Of course, we want everyone to be believed in matters of his conscience on the basis of his own declaration, as long as his deeds do not indicate the opposite. Anyone who in the case of grosser and more serious sins says from his heart, 'I am sorry, I won't do it any more', will along with these words also provide many earnest indications of his repentance; he will also with great humility and eagerness of spirit subject himself to the church's discipline, wanting nothing more than to satisfy the church through his penance [87(Z3)b] and make amends to those whom he has injured through his sin.

Now, since the church does not administer holy baptism to adults on the basis of their word alone, [206] but examines them for a time, as to their lives as well, delaying the baptism to see if they show the beginning of all grace in Christ, in whom they believe; why then should the church immediately administer the holy Supper to someone on the basis of his word alone, and not also require evidence of deeds, when he had given long and substantial evidence of his unbelief not only by what he had said but also by what he had done? This sacrament is as holy as baptism, and should be administered with the same great earnestness and truth as baptism.

The second thing to be maintained here is that, like the ancient holy fathers, I have identified the binding which the Lord commanded to his church with the binding of penance. Pious Christians should consider that the binding commanded by the Lord to his church is nothing other than retaining sins and not pardoning or releasing from them. Therefore it is fitting that the church requires of those responsible for causing grave injury to the church by their grosser sins, evidence of their repentance by prompt penance, before it grants them pardon and restores them to the full communion of Christ; and it may not entirely put aside their sins until they have done penance in this way, and so to this extent retains these sinners in their bonds. And because, as we have previously shown, it does this according to the ordinance and command of Christ, anyone can well see that this temporal binding to penance and satisfaction of the church is also comprised in [88(Z4)a] the binding which the Lord commanded the church. And this binding by the church consists not only in its completely excluding from heaven those who are unbelieving and unrepentant, excluding them entirely from the church of God and binding them to eternal death; but also in that binding by which it temporarily excludes believers from the heavenly fellowship of the church and to a certain degree keeps them away from the communion of Christians, and binds to temporal penance alone. May the Lord grant us to be steadfast in the truth and commit ourselves rightly to his pasture and shelter, counsel and help. Amen.

IO

How the Weak Sheep Are to Be Strengthened

Isaiah 35 [:3f.]

Those who have become timid, so that they must suffer greatly at the hands of the wicked, are to be strengthened by the fact that the Lord is near with his help.

i. *Strengthen the feeble hands, steady the knees that give way; say to those with fearful hearts, 'Be strong, do not fear; your God will come, he will come with vengeance; with divine retribution he will come to save you.'*

[207] Luke 22 [:31f.]

The faith that Christ the Lord is and does everything may in the case of everyone be strengthened, because St Peter himself fell, and the Lord commanded him so insistently to strengthen his brothers.

ii. *The Lord said:* [88(Z4)b] *'Simon, Simon, Satan has asked to sift you as wheat. But I have prayed for you, Simon, that your faith may not fail. And when you have turned back, strengthen your brothers.'*

Romans 14 [:1]

The consciences of those who are still weak and stupid in their understanding of Christ must be truly and very kindly led to a better understanding.

iii. *Accept him whose faith is weak, without confusing consciences.*

1 Thessalonians 5 [:14]

Some are sick and weak in respect of properly ordered lives, others in respect of their faith and hope in God.

iv. *And we urge you, brothers, warn those who are idle, encourage the timid, help the weak, be patient with everyone.*

From these texts we learn what the weaknesses and sicknesses of Christ's sheep are, and how and by whom these are to be treated and the weak sheep strengthened. The identity of the sick and weak sheep we have already briefly indicated. However, the texts we have quoted speak of four sorts of weakness.

Weakness under the cross.

The first of these is that of those who have become timid and weary under the cross and persecution, or through some other accident or offence. This weakness is spoken of in the whole of the first text, and by the words *encourage the timid* in the fourth.

Weakness in confessing Christ.

The second weakness is that of those who do not cling to Christ steadfastly enough and do not always sufficiently [89(a1)a] consider that they have every good thing in Christ alone, and therefore the world's favour and disfavour, advantages and disadvantages, joy and sorrow, honour and shame easily entice them away from confessing Christ and prevent them living a proper Christian life. The second text speaks of this weakness.

Weakness in understanding of Christ.

The third weakness is that of those who do not yet correctly understand Christ's salvation and have not yet attained sufficient knowledge of those things which belong to the Christian life, but still hang on to all sorts of things which are inconsistent with faith in Christ, like those at Rome who were not yet able to regard as alike and use all times and foods to the Lord. Thus in our own times weak ones of this type are those who still pay too much attention to the common ceremonies and outward practices. All this comes from stupidity in understanding of Christ our Lord. This weakness is described in the third text.

Weakness in disorderly living.

The fourth weakness is that of those who do not look steadfastly enough to Christ the Lord in what they do and allow, [208] and are so weak in their contemplation of his will that they easily succumb to the lusts and desires of the flesh; and because they do not live zealously according to their calling and the rule of Christ, they do not serve to anyone's advantage or improvement, but live lives which are dissolute, disorderly and worldly.

All deficiency of life comes from deficiency of faith.

Now, all these weaknesses and sicknesses come from stupidity with regard to the faith and fear of God. Because if someone was properly grounded in faith in Christ our Lord, and believed all his words entirely [89(a1)b] and always considered them, he would have neither the ability nor the desire to do other than love him with all his heart and fear and respect him above all in everything, and also detest and shun above all things those things which incense him. For when someone truly believes the gospel, he can have no doubt that it is Christ the Lord alone who reconciles us to the Father, turning away evil and bestowing all that is good, and that it is he alone who will judge and condemn us, here and in eternity.

Our nature and being have been created in such a way that we desire to live for and to please most of all the one from whom we hope for the most good, and to fear and respect most of all the one whom we recognize to have the greatest power. Therefore, anything which is missing or aberrant in genuine Christian living always comes from the fact that the faith of such Christians is foolish and deficient, with the result that they either do not sufficiently know how they are to commit themselves to Christ our Lord, or do not consider it as seriously as they should.

Those who are still in error with regard to worship do not yet entirely understand Christ.

As for those who are still in error with regard to worship and think that various outward ceremonies and practices are essential for worship, although they are not required by the Lord, like those at Rome who were weak in the faith and are spoken of in the third text: they do not yet understand the gospel aright and do not know completely what is to comfort them in Christ; that is, the fact that he brings salvation by his merit alone, and requires nothing else of them but that [90(a2)a] they steadfastly believe and acknowledge this, and then out of thanksgiving to him be and become to their neighbour everything in order that he, too, may be encouraged to the same faith and be kept and strengthened in it.

All weakness in the Christian life comes from weakness of faith.

But as for those who become weary and timid under the cross, those who are too much attracted to temporal things, so that they either fall away from their confession of Christ and beneficial service of their neighbour, and from the discipline and holiness which are necessary for such service, or else become weary and negligent in these things, who are described in the first, third and fourth [209] texts: these commonly do not consider sufficiently that Christ our Lord alone is the One who is, gives and performs for us everything which we can desire for our true advantage, happiness and honour. For anyone who with true faith would always consider the fact that Christ the Lord alone is the One who is, gives and performs for us everything that we could ever wish or desire, would also know and consider that all tribulation must also contribute towards his blessedness, and that everything, however good it might appear to be, which he enjoys apart from Christ and which is offensive to Christ, is a poison which leads to eternal death, and therefore he would not be fearful or timid in any tribulation. And nothing in the world could happen to him which was either so dreadful or so delightful that because of it he would ever omit to confess and give praise to Christ by word or deed, or be negligent in doing these things, even if he had to suffer many deaths and be deprived of all joys, possessions and honours upon earth.

How the weak sheep are in general to be strengthened.

Therefore, since all sicknesses and weaknesses [90(a2)b] in the Christian life stem from the weakness and stupidity of faith, and faith comes from the word of God and is strengthened and encouraged by it, all strengthening of the weak and ailing sheep depends on the word of God being faithfully set forth to them, and them being led to listen to it gladly and have all their joy in it.

And since the Lord, to promote the right understanding of his holy gospel—from which alone all godliness and blessedness come—has ordained the holy assemblies and practices of the church and has so earnestly commanded his people to flee with utter abhorrence all other activities and to join and commit themselves to these assemblies and practices of the church with heartfelt reverence, with regard to the weak and stupid sheep the most important thing that must be done is to point out to them and warn them that they should attend the assemblies of the church with all diligence, listen eagerly to God's word, receive the holy sacraments, and be zealous and reverent in all the practices of the church.

And so that the word should not fall among the thorns of worldly cares and pleasures, which then choke the seed of God's word, Christ's sheep are also to be earnestly drawn away from such worldly affairs and enjoyments and encouraged to special prayer and constant meditation in the law of God. This will help them to [210] hear and retain the holy gospel of Christ Jesus our Lord with freer and purer hearts, and a more lucid [91(a3)a] and effective understanding, and to consider it more in all their plans, taking it into account in whatever they may be called upon to do or to suffer, and ordering and undertaking everything they do or allow in accordance with it.

When people are lax about church practices there is to be found weakness in their Christian lives.

This is the principal and general way of strengthening the weak and foolish sheep of Christ. Therefore, where there are Christians who are not diligent in attending the church of God and the holy assemblies, and show themselves to be somewhat cool in their attitude towards the blessed practices of the church, praises, prayers, general almsgiving, the sacraments and so on, the most important thing is to make such people joyful and passionate about these godly practices. For even though one may not yet notice any specially disorderly living, nor any special timidity under the cross or valuing the world too highly and Christ too lowly, these weaknesses will without doubt soon appear and break out as soon as offences and objections come. These are also generally those who err in their Christian understanding first in one direction and then in another, because they do not really long to have the mind of Christ.

Now, the particular degrees and forms of weaknesses of Christ's sheep which we will come across are pointed out in the texts which we have quoted. Those who are disorderly the Apostle tells us to warn and admonish, νουθετεῖν. Those who are weak in the faith, that is, in their understanding of Christ, are to be lifted up, and not subjected to searching examination of their thoughts and consciences.

How those who are disorderly are to be strengthened.

[91(a3)b] When someone is living disorderly, not holding on to Christ with all his heart, all his soul and all his strength, and not cultivating all godliness, holiness and love towards his neighbour, neither his mind nor his conscience is right. Therefore such people must have pointed out to them through God's word their failings and errors, their foolishness of mind and conscience, and be directed and led to Christ our Lord, so that they may receive from him a right mind and conscience and in this way be enabled to see and acknowledge that all gain, all enjoyment, all honour apart from Christ is poison and death, but that in Christ all loss is true and eternal gain, joy and honour, even though one may have to live in the world's sight as blessed with troubles and labours, poor and needy, weak and despised.

[211] *How the timid are to be strengthened.*

Those who become timid, so that the cross and tribulation become too heavy for them, must be addressed kindly and comfortingly, faithfully impressing on them the goodness of God and the salvation of Christ, so that they may recognize and believe that our dear God's intentions towards them are entirely fatherly and faithful in all the suffering he sends them. They are always to be dissuaded from thinking about their sins and all unhappiness, and to be uplifted into the mercy of God and the salvation of Christ Jesus.

How the weak are to be strengthened in their understanding of Christ.

Those who still err somewhat in God's service are to be treated with all kindness, and they must be given plenty of scope, and not be called to account about everything, or be overtaxed by untimely arguments, [92(a4)a] which will only confuse them and do nothing at all about the fact that they have still not been given strength. One should praise God that they have got to the point of calling upon Christ as their Saviour, abiding in the church of God, and hearing the word of the Lord; and in addition one should continually strengthen them and encourage them with the fact that Christ the Lord has earned for us forgiveness of our sins by his suffering alone, and that it is his desire that all our diligence and service should be directed to putting to death our evil lusts and desires, living our whole lives for the praise of God and the well-being of our neighbour, and that we must worship him in spirit and in truth; and also that all our outward activities should always be directed to serving God in our neighbour better, in all holiness and righteousness. And when this recognition increases in people, it is then that those fantasies of unbelief whereby they might still err will automatically disappear, and in this way they will also become day by day more capable and fit to have a pure and perfect grasp of the doctrine of Christ.

How those are to be strengthened who have a somewhat greater affection for the world than the Lord desires.

Where there are those who value the world's favour and disfavour too highly, so that they do not acknowledge and praise Christ our Lord and his word joyfully enough, they must always have it clearly impressed upon them that the Father has given Christ our Lord all power and jurisdiction in heaven and on earth, that he alone can and will bestow on us everything that is good and turn away all that is evil, and that the whole world is nothing and can do nothing of itself. And also that on that day [92(a4)b] he will acknowledge before his heavenly [212] Father and his holy angels those who have acknowledged him here before this adulterous world, and will disown those who have disowned him before this world.

By whom the weak sheep are to be strengthened.

So this is how the weak and ailing sheep of Christ are to be strengthened and comforted, and this is to be done by all Christians. For since Christ lives in all his members, he will also exercise this pastoral work of his in all. But because the carers of souls are specially ordained for this purpose, it is fitting that they should also pursue this work of the care of souls before any other, and carry it out most faithfully. Rulers are to see that the churches are provided with carers of souls who are keen and zealous in this work, and perform this work in all weak and foolish sheep, and are to encourage them with all faithfulness, thus also exercising for their part their ministry to Christ the chief Shepherd in this work of helping and strengthening the sick and ailing sheep. So this, as we have said, is all directed at seeing that through the holy gospel of Christ people are well instructed and reminded to seek everything in Christ our Lord alone, and be satisfied with all things in him. So much for the fourth task of the care of souls, the way in which the weak and sick sheep are to be strengthened.

11

How the Healthy and Strong Sheep Are to Be Guarded and Fed

John 21 [:13-17]

Christ's sheep are to be fed and guarded, and their proper care and every need attended to, and they are to be defended against all harm, in such a way that in this work the love of Christ our Lord is shown in the highest degree.

i. *'Simon son of John, do you truly love me more than these?' 'Yes, Lord',*
he said, 'you know that I love you.' Jesus said, 'Feed my lambs.' Again
Jesus said, 'Simon son of John, do you truly love me?' He answered,
'Yes, Lord, you know that I love you.' Jesus said, 'Take care of my sheep.'
The third time he said to him, 'Simon son of John, do you love me?'
Peter was hurt because Jesus asked him the third time, 'Do you love
me?' He said, 'Lord, you know all things; you know that I love you.'
Jesus said, 'Feed my sheep.'

1 Peter 5 [:1-4]

The elders are to feed Christ's lambs with diligent care, willingly, not out
of greed, gently and kindly and giving a good example, as servants of Christ,
not lords over the flock.

ii. *To the elders among you, I appeal as a fellow-elder, a witness of*
Christ's sufferings and one who also will share in the glory to be revealed:
Be shepherds of God's flock that is under your care, serving as over-

seers—not because you must, but because you are willing, as God wants
you to be; not greedy for money, but eager to serve; not lording it over
those entrusted to you, but being examples to the flock. And [213] *when*
the Chief Shepherd appears, you will receive the crown of glory that
will never fade away. [93(b1)b]

Acts 20 [:18-21]

To feed Christ's sheep rightly requires the highest unwavering earnestness
and faithful proclamation of everything which will help in this: teaching and
attestation in general, and in particular repentance towards God and faith in
Christ.

iii. *You know how I lived the whole time I was with you, from the*
first day I came into the province of Asia. I served the Lord with great
humility and with tears, although I was severely tested by the plots of
the Jews. You know that I have not hesitated to preach anything that
would be helpful to you but have taught you publicly and from house to
house. I have declared to both Jews and Greeks that they must turn to
God in repentance and have faith in our Lord Jesus.

Ibid. [:26-28]

The shepherds of Christ's flock are to declare the whole counsel of God faithfully
without keeping anything back, and watch over the flock with the greatest
bravery, so that the wolves are unable to break in.

iv. *Therefore, I declare to you today that I am innocent of the blood*
of all men. For I have not hesitated to proclaim to you the whole will
of God. Keep watch over yourselves and all the flock of which the Holy
Spirit has made you bishops. Be shepherds of the church of God, which
he bought with his own blood.

1 Thessalonians 2 [:5-12]

The pious shepherds must do and suffer everything to commend themselves and the truth of Christ to the people. They must be just like a mother, like a nurse caring for her little children, or a father his sons, warning, comforting and testifying both in general and each one in particular, so that they may live in accordance with their divine calling.

v. *You know we never used flattery, nor did we put on a mask to cover up greed—God is our witness. We were not looking for praise* [94(b2)a] *from men, not from you or anyone else. As apostles of Christ we could have been a burden to you, but we were gentle among you, like a mother caring for her little children. We loved you so much that we were delighted to share with you not only the gospel of God but our lives as well, because you had become so dear to us. Surely you remember, brothers, our toil and hardship; we worked night and day in order not to be a burden to anyone while we preached the gospel of God to you. You are our witnesses, and so is God, of how holy, righteous and blameless we were among you who believed. For you know that we dealt with each of you as a father deals with his own children, encouraging, comforting and urging you to live lives worthy of God, who calls you into his kingdom and glory.*

1 Corinthians 5 [:2]

In order that the healthy sheep should not be corrupted by the wicked goats or mangy sheep, such goats and mangy sheep are to be diligently and promptly put out of the fellowship.

vi. *And you are proud! Shouldn't you rather have been filled with grief and have put out of your fellowship the man who did this?*

Ibid. [:6-7a]

vii. *Your boasting is not good. Don't you know that a* [94(b2)b] *little yeast works through the whole batch of dough? Get rid of the old yeast so that you may be a new batch without yeast.*

[214] Ibid. [:11-13]

viii. *But now I am writing to you that you must not associate with anyone who calls himself a brother but is sexually immoral or greedy, an idolater or a slanderer, a drunkard or a swindler. With such a man do not even eat. What business is it of mine to judge those outside the church? Are you not to judge those inside? God will judge those outside. 'Expel the wicked man from among you.'*

Which sheep are called healthy.

Which are the healthy, strong sheep has been stated above. Although there is no-one free of all defects and weaknesses, those who live in the fear of God, remaining within the church of God, and showing themselves in it to be diligent and keen in the holy practices of the church and in all their Christian life, are described as healthy and strong sheep.

How this work of guarding the healthy sheep is to be carried out in general and specifically by the carers of souls.

These are now to be guarded and fed, that is, protected against all harm and provided with every necessity, as is right, with moderation and order, as the Lord has commanded. All the Lord's members, each according to his calling and ability, are to serve in this work of the Lord, as we [95(b3)a] have already explained concerning the other tasks of the Lord's ministry. Each Christian is to help and counsel the other to the best of his ability, so that he may be protected against all evil and provided with all that is good. But those who are principally to concentrate on this are those who have some authority over others, such as fathers of families, masters of apprentices, and above all civil rulers. But since we are dealing here particularly with the care of souls and the ministry of the spiritual pastoral office which are to be exercised by the ministers of the church, we have only referred to those texts which speak of the guarding and feeding which is to be carried out by the elders of the church. This is what SS Peter and Paul themselves were, as were those whom they admonished about this task in the second and third texts.

When we look at these texts correctly, they teach us very clearly everything that is required in this ministry and how it should be properly carried out. First, we can see here what the goal and objective are of this guarding and feeding. Secondly, we see how and by what means one may approach and achieve this goal and objective. Thirdly, we see how the shepherds and carers of souls must be equipped in order to [215] carry out this task well and achieve their intended objective. Fourthly, we see what motives are to drive and concern them in this.

The goal of proper feeding of Christ's sheep.

Since everything about this task is seen from the viewpoint of its goal and objective, we need first of all to examine this goal and objective. [95(b3)b] This goal and objective are sufficiently set forth in all four texts, but St Paul sets it forth in somewhat clearer and more unequivocal words in the fourth *[fifth]* text, speaking of living and walking according to the grace and calling of God, who *has called us into his kingdom and glory.* For this is the goal and objective of all guarding and feeding of Christ's lambs: that they should be kept and built up in him, that they should live according to the grace of God, who has called them into his kingdom and glory. That is, that they should live and walk as children of God, as members of the kingdom of heaven without fault or defect, in all holiness and righteousness, without offence and filled with the fruit of every good work, as is fitting for children of God and members of Christ.

Those carers of souls who wish to carry out this purpose and this objective faithfully, feeding the lambs of Christ in such a way that they achieve this goal and objective of their feeding, will immediately recognize all this, and also employ the correct knowledge and moderation to carry this out properly and effectively, so that in this way they may effectively minister to Christ's sheep in order that they may not only be kept and guarded in leading proper Christian lives in every way, but also constantly grow and increase. This, then, is the first aspect of the objective and purpose of Christian feeding. How one achieves this objective, which is the second point here, can also be learnt from the first.

Character and nature of faith.

Living in accordance with the gracious calling of the Lord for his [96(b4)a] kingdom and his glory consists entirely in having a true and living faith in our Lord Jesus Christ, from which certainly grow and flourish all discipline, patience and love and thus a complete Christian life and all good works, as we have also already shown. Because when this faith is really living and active in us, we will know and really take note of the fact that as far as our whole nature, ability and deeds are concerned we are under God's wrath and disfavour, as those who in all these things are living eternally in stubborn opposition to God our Creator and the eternal good of ourselves and of all creatures, and are therefore also eternally rejected and condemned by God; but through the satisfaction and merit of our Lord Jesus Christ he, our heavenly Father, [216] desires graciously to pardon and no longer to take into account all this stubbornness against his will (which is only good), and this great unrighteousness and sin and all the transgressions which spring up from this evil root and grow daily; and also to bestow upon us his Spirit, understanding and good will, so that we may always long and strive after a new and godly life. And whatever comes to us in the future, sweet and bitter, good and evil, he will cause everything to serve to the good of our body and soul.

From this it must then follow that we are heartily displeased by our own corrupt nature, our perverse thoughts, lusts and desires, and instead we [96(b4)b] have all our joy, comfort and confidence in him, Christ our Lord. For through this faith he lives in us and we in him, and his Spirit leads us so that for evermore we desire and undertake to crucify and put to death all our natural, foolish and wicked desires, lusts and intentions, and to frame and dedicate our whole lives to the service of our neighbours in true love and to the praise of Christ; with the sole desire that through us his holy name might be magnified and his kingdom extended.

Now, since this Christian and godly life flows entirely from a true and living faith in Christ the Lord, it can be clearly seen that if Christians are to be kept, guarded and encouraged so that they live in accordance with their calling and the grace they have received, i.e. that they live a truly Christian life, it must above all be ensured that they are healthy in the faith and that all their plans, decisions and actions stem from faith and a living knowledge of Christ, that they always take good account of and consider what Christ has become, done and given for us, and what he will be, do and give for us. Thus St Paul, when he prays for believers to progress in the Christian life, prays constantly that they might grow and increase and be filled with spiritual wisdom, revelation and knowledge, enlightenment, understanding and insight, so that they might recognize and feel and conclude what our hope and rich inheritance are, which have been won for us by Christ; and following on from that, what is pleasing to God, [97(c1)a] what is truly useful and good, so that they might live in accordance with their calling and to the praise of the Lord, without offence and filled with all the fruits of righteousness, Eph. 1 [:16ff.], Phil. 1 [:9ff.], Col. 1 [:9ff.]. In this way *the faith from the hearing* [Rom. 10:17] of God's word will first be born, and then grow and be strengthened, and thus from looking at this objective and purpose of the true care of souls and proper feeding we learn the second point: by what means one reaches this objective and achieves this purpose. This is anything which helps pious carers of souls to do everything necessary in order that Christ's healthy [217] sheep may be taught ever more perfectly in the holy gospel, and that the whole counsel of God may be always faithfully proclaimed to them by teaching, admonishing, convincing and anything else, so that the knowledge of Christ in believers may grow and become stronger.

And so that this work in Christ's sheep might be better achieved, they must by all means and with the greatest diligence and earnestness be encouraged, led and prompted, both generally and particularly, to turn from all worldly and carnal affairs and lusts to all spiritual and heavenly deeds and activities. For this we have the example of St Paul in the third and fifth texts. He withheld from Christ's sheep which he was commanded to feed nothing at all which is helpful, and he declared the whole counsel of God to them, and taught, comforted, [97(c1)b] admonished and convinced them, all together in the congregation and specially in their homes, each one individually. This teaching is a form of instruction including everything necessary to enable someone to be encouraged more and more to understand the things of God aright [νουθετεῖν], in order that he might come to be a Christian and to live a Christian life. Conviction is that most earnest admonition by which the believing heart is most vehemently searched and moved. This is something which St Paul strove for without ceasing, day and night, with tears; such was the earnestness and concern that he demonstrated, devoting all his power, all his efforts and labours to teach them about repentance towards God and faith in our Lord Jesus.

The doctrine of Christ must be proclaimed not only in the pulpit, but also in the home and to each one individually.

But in this matter it is specially to be noted that the doctrine of Christ is to be faithfully proclaimed not only in the public gatherings of the church, but also in the home and to each one individually, following the example of Paul in the third and fifth texts. Thus in the third text he states: *I have proclaimed the doctrine of Christ to you and taught you in the general and public assembly,* δημοσίᾳ— *and also privately from house to house,* κατ᾽ οἴκους. And afterwards: *For three years I never stopped warning each of you day and night.* And in the [218] fifth text: *Like a father his children I have warned each one of you &c.* The doctrine of the holy gospel is the doctrine of eternal salvation, and on account of our corrupt nature there is nothing more difficult and troublesome for us to learn; that is why this doctrine requires the most faithful, earnest and persistent teaching, [98(c2)a] instruction and admonition that anyone could ever employ. But everyone knows full well what other instruction and admonition people may be receiving in private.

This is why Christian doctrine and admonition must not be confined to the assembly and the pulpit; because there are very many people who will take what they are taught and admonished in the public gathering as being of only general application, and consider it to apply more to others than to themselves. Therefore it is essential that people should also be instructed, taught and led on in Christ individually in their homes. That is why those churches have acted wisely which have retained the individual approach to teaching repentance and faith to each one who is in Christ the Lord. And those who wish to hinder all ministers of Christ everywhere from dispensing and proclaiming Christ's doctrine not only in public and general sermons but also from house to house, to each one individually, are opposing the Holy Spirit and fighting against the reformation of the church. That in the case of St Paul this was the work of the Holy Spirit is clear to see; and if the Holy Spirit worked through dear Paul for the reformation of his church, why should he not also work through all his other instruments who have been thus called and commanded?

But our treacherous and unruly flesh always wants to give the impression of also wanting to be a pupil of Christ, when in fact there is nothing it will tolerate less than Christ's doctrine. That is why it would be happy for Christ's doctrine to be left as a general statement which may or may not apply. But it is not possible for the [98(c2)b] Spirit of Christ to leave it like that: he is a faithful Teacher who will not give up until he has led his pupils into all truth. Therefore he also looks from house to house, from person to person, to see how his lesson by means of public and general sermons has been received, what they have learned from them, and examines his pupils to see what they have or have not grasped. That has always been his practice in his church; and anyone who does not like it and does not wish to restore it to use does not want the Holy Spirit to [219] teach his church properly and to be its true Patron and Teacher, as the Lord promised he would be. Paul writes to the Thessalonians that it is like a father that he has warned each one of them &c. We should ask the Lord for ministers like this, and wherever we can we should reintroduce and encourage such a ministry. And if otherwise we are Christians and are led by his Spirit, this too we will do with all faithfulness.

So this is what must be done for Christ's sheep if we wish to feed and guard them correctly, that is, lead and encourage them rightly so that they live in accordance with their calling and the grace they have received. We must endeavour, undertake and carry out everything to do with them with the greatest diligence and earnestness, both generally and also particularly to individuals in their homes, so that in this way they may be encouraged to grow and increase constantly in the faith and knowledge of Christ, and that everything by which they might be drawn away from or prevented from following the only way may be removed from them. [99(c3)a]

CONCERNING THE EXCLUSION AND
SEPARATION OF THE FALSE GOATS

A further consequence of this is that it is not only necessary to guard against and remove the hindrances and offences which may be brought upon themselves by Christ's healthy sheep, which allow themselves to be kept in the Christian pasture; but also to protect those which may be attacked by the mangy sheep and false goats which disguise themselves for a time in sheep's clothing. This is the subject of the last three texts.

Bad examples are not to be tolerated in any upright congregation.

A little yeast works through the whole batch of dough [Gal. 5:9]. One mangy sheep soon infects a whole flock. That is why the Lord also commanded so earnestly that evil and wicked people should be removed and driven out from the people of God, Deut. 13 [:2ff.], 17 [:2ff.], and in other places. He also taught this to all people by the light of nature. For wherever there are or have been properly ordered cities, households and other upright communities, those who do not want to behave according to the rules of those communities by living an upright, industrious, decent and honourable life will not be tolerated, but will be excluded, either being banished for a time if some improvement is hoped for, or if no such improvement is hoped for or the crime is so great that it demands such a strict penalty, banished for ever. Indeed, if their wickedness is too great, they are removed from human society completely [99(c3)b] and put to death. We are [220] always more inclined to pursue the wicked than the good, because when we have a bad example set before us, it will not go away without a great deal of trouble. But the pious shepherds are to do all in their power faithfully to destroy and turn away all offences from Christ's sheep.

Those who should be excluded.

This is why, as well as the faithful teaching, admonishing and convincing to lead a godly life which the pious shepherds are to carry out publicly and with individuals, it is also necessary in order to guard the healthy sheep and feed them in the right way for the carers of souls to exercise the greatest earnestness for the good of the congregation to exclude and keep away from it all those who refuse to listen to the church when they are warned in its name to repent, amend their ways and seek what is good, but instead wish to persist in their disorderly lives, and do not want to do good according to their calling and conduct themselves in obedience to the holy gospel and lead a Christian life, but fall into serious sins and lusts and refuse to repent, or become rebellious and start up gangs and sects.

All these are to be excluded from the congregations, as the word of God expressly shows in Matthew 18 [:17]: *Regard him as a heathen and a publican;* do not eat and drink with them, 1 Corinthians 5 [:11]; have no fellowship with them, 2 Thessalonians 3 [:14]. Now, it is not possible for the word and doctrine of God to teach and command anything which is not possible, helpful, good and beneficial.

How those who have been excluded are to be regarded.

But those who are [100(c4)a] excluded must be handled with restraint if there is any hope that they may eventually be brought to repentance, so that even while they are excluded one should not neglect to take every opportunity to admonish them to repent. Just as a shepherd does not immediately reject the mangy sheep which he has separated from the healthy ones, until he has tried out every medicine on them; but he gives them this medicine in a special place, and does not leave them among the other healthy sheep.

The matter of the excommunication for penance and humiliation of those who have sinned but want to mend their ways has been dealt with under the third point in the chapter on how the wounded sheep are to be healed. But as for those who do not want to take any notice when they are admonished to mend their ways, they must be completely excluded, not just excommunicated for a time. We may pray for them as the Holy Spirit leads, and if we feel there are grounds for doing so, urge them to repent; otherwise, however, we are to have nothing to do with them, and they are to be shown with Christian severity how greatly we condemn and abhor their ungodliness.

[221] But since we are to be like our heavenly Father and do good to all people, including our enemies; and since the just God who is to the highest degree the enemy of all that is evil yet causes his sun to shine and his rain to fall even on the wicked, unrighteous and ungrateful [Matt. 5:45], and richly provides them with bodily sustenance and everything necessary for this life, we who are his children must also, as long as we live among the wicked in this world, not withhold or refuse any good deed necessary for their well-being. [100(c4)b] But we must distance ourselves from their ungodly deeds, and by withdrawing from close association with them show and demonstrate that we are those to whom their ungodly deeds are a great grievance and abomination; and that therefore we do not wish to associate with them any more than is required to meet their needs, because they have thus rejected the fellowship of Christ.

This ban does not hinder civil or natural association.

For when the holy apostle writes: *You are not to have anything to do with them* or eat with them [1 Cor. 5:11], he only wishes to forbid that association in eating and other activities which is voluntary, not that which is required by the general needs of nature, citizenship or domestic relationships.

Thus all honourable people will relinquish and avoid anything approaching real friendship with those belonging to them who defile the relationship with ignominious stains by their dissolute morals. However, such honourable people and relatives will still have dealings with those whom otherwise they avoid in those things which are required by civil society and general human needs, and join with them in doing those things generally required of them by authority, even though it means eating with them, dealing with other things, making, buying and selling, and helping them in case of need. But apart from this they do not maintain friendly relations with them or have anything to do with them, avoid their company, and show in everything displeasure and disapproval of their dissolute and dishonourable ways. And this is how [101(d1)a] Christians are also to behave towards those who have been excluded from the church of God. And if they do this in such a way that they faithfully provide those who have been excluded with everything required by civil society and the general needs of human nature, then those excommunicated people have no reason to blame believers for the fact that they [222] have nothing to do with them in those other things which are voluntary, in which no-one is obliged to another by civil laws. Therefore this avoiding in itself has no other purpose than that such unchristian people should be sooner ashamed of themselves and moved to repentance; for in other ways they experience from believers all fairness, love and goodwill, except in that one thing: that they can have no pleasure in their ungodliness, but must be filled with sorrow and abhorrence, because the

Lord Christ is and means everything to them. Thus Christians exclude no-one except those who wish to persist in public and conscious wrongdoing; therefore such exclusion and avoiding should not be considered either by themselves or by others as an expression of improper contempt. And where truly godly policies are observed, in accordance with the imperial statutes and the ancient Christian practice those who have been excommunicated by the church will also be dealt with as they deserve in the civil sphere. By also being excluded and shunned in civil society at the behest of the authorities they will be encouraged to mend their ways; for heathens among Christians are to be regarded as heathens.

How Christians are to regard their non-Christian relatives.

[101(d1)b] If anyone has relatives living with him who have been excluded from the church of God, so that he has an non-Christian spouse, parents, child or some other relative, no believer can avoid such in eating, drinking, or other outward activities; rather the believing spouse is to behave and show himself towards the unbelieving partner in the whole relationship of marriage, which is the highest of all human activities, in the friendliest way, so that he will be more likely to win his unbelieving spouse to the Lord, 1 Corinthians 7 [:13f.]. In the same way everyone is to behave towards his relations in all the various blood and family relationships. What God has joined together in this or other callings, let not man put asunder.

St Paul did not say about such relatives: *You are not to have anything to do with them,* you are not to eat with them. He did not want in this way to ruin people's ordinary relationships, because Christians are to serve and do good to those who are wicked as well. Therefore, just as he warns slaves that they are to serve their masters faithfully even if they are unbelievers, and those who are married that they are to be diligent in being faithful and loving in marriage towards their unbelieving partner, so also he desires that children, parents and others related by blood or marriage should behave towards one another in accordance with their relationship.

[223] This is all in order that believers may demonstrate their godly grievance, abhorrence and concern about the corruption of [102(d2)a] unbelievers in a Christian and beneficial way, without doing harm to God's calling to particular relationships. First, in this way such believers will not be associated in the sins of unbelievers, but be heartily sorry for them. Secondly, they will on the contrary be all the more zealous and earnest in continuing to do what is right, and by their good life they will condemn the wicked lives of their relatives and make them loathsome to them. Thirdly, whenever they have the opportunity they will request and admonish their relatives to amend their lives with the greatest earnestness, with asking and pleading, even with tears.

Where there is some superiority, as of the husband over his wife, the father or mother over their children, the master over his servants, or older friends over younger ones, those believers in that position of superiority will show their dislike for this ungodly life also by being less approving and accommodating, by withdrawing special friendship and pleasures, or by being more severe in everything, and being quicker and stricter in imposing punishment. But all these things they will apply to a degree which will be beneficial and helpful in enabling people to repent, without doing harm to the calling of God in their relationships and in that way making what is bad even worse.

But for those who are in subordinate positions in these callings, such as wives, children, servants and young friends, their agony with crying, asking and pleading before God and their relatives who are living in an unchristian way will often bring about in these relatives a remarkable [102(d2)b] change for the better from their ruinous state. Thus Christians will always be careful that wickedness should not become an example or something to be followed or become less loathsome, but that it should be more and more abhorred, shunned and detested, and yet that no God-ordained relationship should break down in its obligations, or be hurt in any way. This is to be faithfully promoted by carers of souls by means of timely exclusion from the church of Christ, so that they may protect the healthy sheep from the defilement and legacy of evil, and be better able to lead them on to all good things.

So this is what faithful carers of souls are to undertake and practise so that they may sooner and more perfectly achieve the objective given to them of Christian feeding. They are constantly to remind Christ's lambs with the greatest faithfulness and earnestness of Christ's salvation and to instruct them in what this salvation brings us, and to declare the whole counsel of God, [224] teaching, admonishing and convincing in general and in particular, in the church, in homes, and wherever the people may be found; and in this way always seeking that faith and amendment of life might constantly be promoted among them and increase and grow. And then with great earnestness they are to put out and exclude the mangy sheep and wicked false goats from the true and healthy sheep, so that such unpleasant people should not corrupt others to their ways. This is the second point which we are to learn from the texts we have quoted, concerning how the carers of souls are to achieve the objective they have been given.

What skills and knowledge are required by carers of souls in order to feed the sheep correctly.
Love for Christ and the sheep.

The third point, what sort of people carers of souls need to be, [103(d3)a] what skills they must have and what knowledge and measures they must employ in order to carry out this task of theirs in this way, we are also very clearly and fully taught in the texts we have quoted. In the first place, they must love Christ the Lord with all their hearts, with that love which the Lord required of Peter when he commanded him to feed his lambs, as the first text teaches. An immediate consequence of this love will be true love for Christ's flock. Towards that flock they must have a heart which is truly that of a father and mother, as St Paul testifies of himself in the fifth text. They must aim for and seek nothing other than the salvation of the sheep, showing by their actions that this is their inclination and their heart's desire. This they must do in such a way that the children of God see that they are ready and anxious to share with them not only the gospel, but also their own souls and lives; and that the sheep are their love and the joy of their hearts, as also exemplified by Paul in the fifth text. Where there is this feeling of love and affection for the flock, the carers of souls are sure to carry out this ministry of theirs without compulsion but voluntarily, and without thought of gain or honour but gladly, as St Peter exhorts the elders to do in the second text. Again St Paul sets before us his own example in the third and fifth texts.

Where this is the case it will certainly result in such carers of souls, given the opportunity and ability, being far more happy to work day and night with their own hands, as St Paul did, rather than to become a burden to someone in the church. But if they do not have that opportunity [103(d3)b] and ability and have to take advantage of the right given to them by Christ our Lord (which can never really be a burden to believers) to reap their material needs from those [225] among whom they have sown spiritual seed, taking their food from those among whom they have laboured with the holy gospel—even if in Paul's words they are worthy of double honour, such as the churches have for a long time had an abundance of—so that no-one anywhere should be placed under the least burden on account of providing for faithful ministers who labour in the word and doctrine, they must show themselves to be so thrifty and contented, so gentle towards those who are in need, that all honest people must see that in their ministry they are seeking no gain for themselves, but only the salvation of souls.

A further consequence of this genuine love for Christ and his flock will be that carers of souls will show themselves to be not overbearing or unfriendly, but entirely humble and like a mother, *like a nurse caring for her little child;* thus they will conduct themselves in a proper and friendly way towards people, showing themselves in all their ministry to be cheerful and indefatigable, however badly their ministry may sometimes be received. For this reason they will also take great care to show that their lives are in every respect blameless, righteous and holy, and to be an example to the flock, as we are told by the first *[second]* and fifth texts.

There is no ministry more subject to ingratitude and rebellion than that of the care of souls.

On account of all this they will also suffer and bear all kinds of opposition and persecution with steadfastness and bravery, whether they come from within or without, as we [104(d4)a] learn from the examples of Christ the Lord, Paul, Peter, and other true shepherds of Christ's sheep. For just as there is no task more necessary and beneficial than that of the true and faithful care of souls, so there is no task which should be more highly guarded, and against which Satan is given more leeway in his desire to destroy it; and he is permitted to pursue this work most enthusiastically and persistently not only through his own members, the notorious enemies of believers and the secret traitors who still remain in the church, but also through weak and fragile brothers, and yet not to have any success except with the children of corruption. This is why these ministers must be specially witnesses of Christ's sufferings, [226] as Peter writes concerning himself, and more than others must be patient and suffer much abuse, and always preach the gospel of the cross while themselves bearing the cross and suffering great conflict, as Paul teaches in the third and fifth texts. So now we see what carers of souls are to be like, what knowledge and measures they are to employ, if they want to carry out their ministry and work properly and in this way achieve their objective of feeding Christ's flock correctly.

Now the fourth thing which carers of souls need, and which they must receive for this whole task, is also clearly shown to us in the texts we have quoted. But the main thing, which by itself should be sufficient for all pious carers of souls, is the most earnest command of Christ: when St Peter is asked for the third time if he loves the Lord, and himself for the third time protests his love, then for the third time the Lord [104(d4)b] says to him: *Feed my sheep.* It is as if he were saying: If you love me so much and want to show this by your actions, feed my sheep, because there is nothing you can do for me which is preferable or more pleasing to me.

If we really love Christ, he is everything to us; therefore if anyone is called to this ministry, whatever unpleasantness, sufferings and crosses he may have to bear in the course of his ministry, he will be upheld and strengthened against all unpleasantness, sufferings and crosses only by the fact that the Lord Jesus has commanded him to do this, and commanded it as the highest ministry of love that we can show him. Then each one will feel as Paul did when he writes about himself in 1 Corinthians 9 [:16f.]: *Yet when I preach the gospel, I cannot boast, for I am compelled to preach. Woe to me if I do not preach the gospel! If I preach voluntarily, I have a reward; if not voluntarily, I am simply discharging the trust committed to me.*

I am simply discharging the trust committed to me, says the dear apostle; for that should be more than enough for any Christian, if he is called to this ministry, to accept it and carry it out with all faithfulness, withstanding and suffering whatever trouble, labour, abuse, shame, suffering and cross he may meet in the course of it.

For the Lord will require the blood of his lambs at the hands of all those who either do not accept this ministry when they are called to it, or are in some way neglectful in it. This is why St Paul says to the Ephesians: *I declare to you today* [105(c1)a] *that I am innocent of the blood of all men. For I have not deprived you of anything* [227] *&c.* In this way he recognizes that if in any way he had been neglectful and deprived them of anything, he would have made himself guilty of their blood.

But there is so much and such delightful consolation for us in the fact that in this way we are showing the greatest love to our Lord Jesus, by serving him in his dear church which he has purchased with his precious blood, which is his dear spouse and his body. This is the substance of the fourth text.

May the Lord grant that this should be well considered and examined, and that he should be faithfully followed, by all those who are already in the ministry of the care of souls, or who are yet to be called to it, in order that Christ's lambs may be well guarded and fed as they should be. That concludes our consideration of the fifth and final task of the care of souls.

May the Lord Jesus, our chief Shepherd and Bishop, grant us such elders and carers of souls as will seek his lambs which are still lost, bring back those which have wandered, heal those which are wounded, strengthen those which are sickly, and guard and feed in the right way those which are healthy, in the way we have described. Those who are sheep and not goats will allow themselves to be brought by such carers of souls and ministers of Christ through the word of the Lord into Christ's church and into his sheep-fold, and to be kept in it, healed, strengthened, guarded and fed, in all things obeying and gladly following him. For anyone who is born of God hears his word, and Christ's sheep [105(c1)b] hear his word and follow him.

How Satan makes the most faithful carers of souls more than any others insulted, suspected and despised by the sheep.

But because Satan knows that this hearing and following is important for the sheep's whole salvation, he does his very best to awaken in the sheep some displeasure, mistrust and unruliness towards those who are supposed to lead and feed them by bringing them their Shepherd's voice and teaching. In the whole of the Lord's house there was no-one more faithful and more diligent and keen in serving the people of God than Moses, but Satan managed to arrange that not only the foolish people grumbled and rebelled against him, and not only the gangs of Korah, Dathan and Abiram rose up against him, but he was also opposed by his own brother, Aaron, and his own sister, Miriam, even though they were holy people, chosen by God and highly talented. And because there was no-one in Christendom who worked harder and more fruitfully than St Paul, there was [228] no other apostle whom Satan attacked so vehemently and whom he so desired to make the object of suspicion and detestation, in the eyes not only of the ordinary Christians, but also of the leaders in Jerusalem and others. It was not only the Galatians, who had otherwise welcomed him as if he were an angel, or even Christ himself, but all those in Asia who had turned away from him, and he had great trouble in looking after the Corinthians.

Those who are not prepared to tolerate the yoke of the holy gospel from the true ministers soon become subject to the yoke of the antichrists.

Thus it has always turned out that the more faithful the carers of souls have been in the exercise of their pastoral ministry, the more Satan has aroused disobedience against them, not only in the [106(e2)a] goats, but also among the immature sheep. And on the other hand he arranges for the foolish sheep then to commit themselves entirely and completely to unfaithful and false shepherds, and to suffer and tolerate from them whatever they ask of them. This is what befell even the clever and spiritually rich Corinthians, so that dear Paul writes to them in 2 Corinthians 11 [:20]: *You even put up with anyone who enslaves you or exploits you or takes advantage of you or defies you or slaps you in the face.*

At this time too, how many there are who want to be counted as excellent Christians, who will not tolerate any punishment or discipline in the Lord at the hands of their faithful ministers of the gospel, but are quick to submit themselves to the leaders of sects and accept all manner of violence and sheer tyranny at their hands, out of the Lord. We have in mind also all those who may in some way have been God-fearing but have had such a high regard for the popish leaders (who were almost all blind leaders of the blind, and most of them deliberate seducers) and have placed so much value on their words and commands, but now are so concerned that they should not have too high an opinion of their ministers in the holy gospel or follow them too much, although those ministers want nothing more than to place upon them the blessed yoke of Christ. Whatever the ministers advise them or bring before them, even though it comes clearly from the Lord's word, they reject, as if it would be tantamount to a denial of Christianity were they to [229] submit themselves in some way to follow or obey it in the [106(e2)b] Lord and not carry on living and acting free of any discipline or punishment according to their own carnal desires.

How to escape from human bondage.

There is nothing which Christians on earth should more diligently guard against, than that anyone should place a strange yoke on them in the name of Christ. We have been purchased by Christ our Lord, and therefore we are to make sure that we do not become the slaves of men, 1 Corinthians 7 [:23]. By this purchase we are Christ's lambs, we are his one church and congregation, and therefore we must also have the Lord's teachers and ministers, whom we listen to in his name and follow with great humility, obedience and submissiveness. This is because it is the Lord's will to rule among us through his appointed ministry, as we have explained in the second and third main chapters of this little book.

Against thoughtless and wanton criticism of teaching.

This is why Christians are first of all to ask the Lord with great earnestness to grant them faithful ministers, and to watch diligently in choosing them to see that they walk in accordance with their calling and serve faithfully; and when these ministers come to warn, punish, teach or exhort in the Lord's name, not to dismiss it thoughtlessly and despise this ministry, as sadly many are wont to do today. Such people are so kind as to object to and judge the sermons and all the church activities of their ministers, just as if they had been appointed to do so and the only reason for hearing sermons was so that they might in the most unfriendly way discuss, distort and run down what had been said in them, or anything else which had been done in the church. In such people you do not observe any thought of approaching sermons [107(e3)a] in such a way that they might in some way be moved by what they have heard in them to acknowledge their sins more fully, or to commit themselves more wholeheartedly to Christ and seek more earnestly to improve their ways; all they do is to judge and criticize anything which is said which applies to them, or which in some way they consider not to fit in with their carnal impudence (and not Christian freedom). And when they praise something in a sermon, it is generally because it applies to other people, whom they like to hear criticized; and they take from such sermons nothing beyond an excuse to run down those they do not like, and not so that they might be warned or built up.

It is true that everything must be examined in order that only what is good should be accepted and retained, but that must be done not thoughtlessly and impudently without regard to love or honour, but in the fear of God, with earnest prayer and genuine humility. Then everyone would take into account his own weakness and ignorance, would value very highly the ordinance and gifts of the *[230]* Lord through his ministers, and would judge them according to their love and the precious worth of their ministry. If he heard or learned something which did not seem good to him, he would be glad to go in love and trust to speak about it with the ministers, pointing out in a friendly way what has offended him, and receiving a further explanation. And he would not condemn as unchristian anything that he had not entirely understood. Then the Lord would grant to us that no-one would deceive us by means of sheep's clothing and false appearances into false doctrine or hypocrisy of life. And in this way all disorder, all impudent criticism, disobedience and contempt of the Lord in his [107(e3)b] ministry would be prevented. If the churches were provided with elders like those we have described above in the fifth chapter of this little book, chosen from all kinds of honourable, God-fearing, well tested and really keen people, it would be very easy for all those who possessed something of the Spirit of Christ to distance themselves and turn away from hastily suspecting, judging or despising Christ's ministry in doctrine, correction and discipline.

In order that believers might also consider well and take to heart what heart-felt love and faithfulness, humility and obedience they should have and show, not to the ministers, but to Christ our Lord in his ministers, in the ministry of their own eternal salvation; and what a great and horrible evil it is to value Christ's ministers so little and to oppose them, judge them and despise them so thoughtlessly; I want to finish this little book by introducing some further texts.

12

Concerning the Obedience of Christ's Sheep

Deuteronomy 17 [:10-13]

Where there is not order and obedience, and that according to God's word, no good can come of it. Therefore it is God's will that anyone who destroys this order and obedience should not live.

i. *You must act according to the decisions they give you at the place the Lord will choose. Be careful to do everything they direct you to do. Act according to the law they teach you and the decisions they give you.* [108(e4)a] *Do not turn aside from what they tell you, to the right or to the left. The man who shows contempt for the judge or for the priest who stands ministering there to the Lord your God must be put to death. You must purge the evil from Israel. All the people will hear and be afraid, and will not be contemptuous again.*

Hosea 4 [:4-6]

When the priest, that is the one who brings God's word, is spoken against, all wisdom and good must fall away, and the people come to nothing at all.

ii. *But let no man bring a charge, let no man accuse another, for your people are like those who bring charges against a priest. You stumble day and night, and the prophets stumble with you.* [231] *So I will destroy your mother* (that is, the whole people)—*my people are destroyed for lack of knowledge. Because you have rejected knowledge, I also reject you as my priests; because you have ignored the law of your God, I also will ignore your children.*

Luke 10 [:16]

We are to look to the One whose word it is, not to the one who brings it.

iii. *He who listens to you listens to me; he who rejects you rejects me; but he who rejects me rejects him who sent me.*

Galatians 4 [:13-16]

Because the Galatians looked not to the weak instrument, Paul, but to the word itself and the Lord whose word it was, they were blessed, and also there was no-one dearer or more precious to them than Paul, who brought this word to them.

[108(e4)b] iv. *As you know, it was because of an illness that I first preached the gospel to you. Even though my illness was a trial to you, you did not treat me with contempt or scorn. Instead, you welcomed me as if I was an angel of God, as if I were Christ Jesus himself. What has happened to your joy? I can testify that, if you could have done so, you would have torn out your eyes and given them to me. Have I now become your enemy by telling you the truth?*

1 Thessalonians 5 [:12f.]

The flesh, which cannot bear correction or teaching, hates carers of souls because of their work and is opposed to them. Therefore the Spirit urges love and peace to be shown to them.

v. *Now we ask you, brothers, to respect those who work hard among you, who are over you in the Lord and who admonish you. Hold them in highest regard in love because of their work, and be at peace with them.*

2 Timothy 4 [:1-5]

Obedience to the holy gospel is to be maintained with great earnestness, because there is nothing that the devil and proud flesh oppose so vehemently. And people always want to have teachers and prohets who will not chide them, but tell them what they like to hear.

> vi. *In the presence of God and of the Lord Jesus Christ, who will come again to judge the living and the dead with his appearing and his kingdom, I give you this charge: preach the word; be prepared in season and out of season; correct, rebuke and encourage—with great patience and careful instruction. For the time will come when men will not put up with sound doctrine. [109(f1)a] Instead, to suit their own desires, they will gather around them a great number of teachers to say what their itching ears want to hear. They will turn their ears from the truth and turn aside to myths. But you, keep your head in all situations, endure hardship, do the work of an evangelist, discharge all the duties of your ministry.*

Titus 2 [:15]

With all gravity, that is, like a ruler towards his subjects, μετὰ πάσης ἐπιταγῆς.

vii. *Teach these things, and encourage and rebuke with all authority. Do not let anyone despise you.*

Hebrews 13 [:17]

Those who distress pious carers of souls with their disobedience do harm to themselves most of all. Those who are truly godly, however, recognize that their salvation is being sought and that it is God's command, and obey; and in doing so they benefit themselves and gladden their carers of souls.

viii. *Obey your teachers and follow them. They keep watch over you as men who must give an account. Obey them so that their work will be a joy, not a burden, for that would be of no advantage to you.*

[232] Anyone approaching these and similar texts with a godly disposition would thoroughly understand how very essential complete obedience in the church of Christ is, and would also desire with all his heart to offer it. For these texts show us very clearly and solemnly that obedience and respect on the part of the congregation towards those who are put over them to teach and discipline them are absolutely essential in the church; and that here the most complete obedience and the greatest respect are commanded.

That obedience in the church is essential.

[109(f1)b] The following reason why obedience and respect towards leaders are absolutely essential will be more than sufficient for all believers: the Lord demands this so earnestly; because he will not allow to live among his people someone who does not obey the priest, as the first text shows; and the second text shows that he rejected his people Israel and made them as nothing, because they despised the priest's correction and stubbornly opposed the priest. And the third shows that anyone who despises ministers of the word despises him and the Father.

Indeed, this very clear indication of God's will and command should be sufficient reason for all believers to recognize that it is absolutely essential that believers should obey the ministers of Christ, who oversee the Christian pasture, and should subject themselves entirely to the Lord's word which these ministers declare to them. The Lord never commands us or requires of us anything except that which is actually useful and necessary for our salvation. From the fact that he so solemnly commands and requires that obedience which is to be offered to the ministers of his word and discipline that if anyone does not listen to these his ministers, he will regard this as nothing other than contempt for himself, and does not want such a one to live among his flock, and because of such disobedience will completely reject his people and make them as nothing; every Christian can easily see that such obedience and subjection in all things are essential, and that without them no-one can belong to God's people, nor escape from God's eternal wrath and punishment.

In all teaching, but particularly teaching concerning life, those who are to learn must think highly of their teachers and have great confidence in them.

[110(f2)a] And when the Christian has first laid upon his heart this true ground of faith, the most earnest command and ordinance of the Lord, and then goes on to see how the Lord has given us such varying gifts of understanding and goodwill, and how he wishes to use us as members of one another, so that one will always teach and build up another in all [233] things; and also that those who are to learn must always believe and trust in their teachers and follow them; then from this he will also see the great necessity for this obedience and respect which there must be in the church on the part of the whole congregation towards their elders and carers of souls, if God's true kingdom is to remain and to grow.

There are so many simple and ignorant people who do not know how to rule and govern themselves according to their own understanding. And because we are all too fond of ourselves, we are not able to recognize or judge our own deeds properly. Therefore, if we do not have a good and high opinion of those whom the Lord has placed over us, and who are to instruct, exhort, admonish and correct us on his behalf, and do not immediately receive their words and teaching with all fear and trembling as the Lord's own words and teaching, then we will get nowhere and will not progress in the pursuit of godliness, as is our current and daily experience.

For where there is not this regard and respect for ministers, we also see that there will be no true church growing in godliness, and that is bound to be the case; because it is the Lord's will to govern his church through his ministers, as we have seen in the third main chapter. [110(f2)b] Those who listen to them listen to him, and those who despise them despise him and the Father. Those who thus despise God and Christ the Lord are rebelling against the One who has made us and purchased us with his blood; this means that the devil is exercising his tyranny, and there can be no other consequence than what the Lord declares to his people in the second text, and St Paul prophesies in the sixth.

This consequence is that all knowledge of the truth departs from the people, and that they do not want to put up with the truth, and invite those who will tickle their ears with false and flattering doctrine; God's law is completely forgotten by them, and they are completely rejected and destroyed by God; this is what happened to the Jews, and later on to so many people in Syria, Egypt, Asia, Greece, Africa and other countries, where there had one been glorious churches, but now the desolate abomination of the Mohammedans reigns, together with other wretched and pernicious sects and heresies, with all manner of physical tyranny and wretched servitude.

It is also because this obedience is so greatly necessary and beneficial to Christians that St Paul so diligently and solemnly commands Timothy and Titus in the sixth and seventh texts, and also elsewhere [234] in the epistles written to these young disciples of his, that they are to insist faithfully on this obedience, not allowing themselves to be despised, with all earnestness and authority like rulers towards their subjects (this is what is meant by μετὰ πάσης ἐπιταγῆς), managing and ordering, delegating and scolding, according to what is best for each individual. [111(f3)a] From all this we recognize very clearly the necessity for this obedience.

That there should be perfect obedience in the church.

All the texts which we have quoted teach that this obedience should be a perfect one, and this respect for all the ministers of Christ should be of the highest character, if the Christian faith is to be rightly maintained and Christ's congregations are to be ordered in a Christian way. We are created by the Lord in such a way that we will yield do, obey and follow the more gladly and entirely, and have a higher opinion of and respect for, those who teach, counsel and command us, insofar as we are taught, counselled and commanded those things which are more useful and beneficial to us, on behalf of in the name of either higher and more powerful masters or dearer and more faithful friends.

And there can be nothing more beneficial and blessed put or commanded to us than what is taught and commanded us by the true ministers of our Lord Jesus Christ. And there is no-one higher or more powerful, or who loves us more genuinely, than our Lord Jesus. So what more perfect obedience and complete surrender, what higher respect and more precious estimation could there be, than what must be shown to Christ the Lord in his ministers by all those who truly confess him as their Saviour and have a right regard to his word: *He who listens to you listens to me?* For whose command could we treasure more highly and accept more gladly than his who in this way desires to call and lead us from eternal death to eternal life [Luke 10:16]?

[113(f3)b] Indeed, if this was thought about and believed, however weak and insignificant according to the flesh the ministers of the care of souls might be, they would nonetheless be received as Paul was by the Galatians, as the angels and messengers of God, which they are, and even as Christ the Lord himself, because he himself speaks and acts through them and wishes to be recognized and acknowledged in them.

The service and love which pious Christians desire to show to their faithful ministers in the Lord.

A further consequence of this is such a love and high estimation of ministers that someone who feels like that will in every respect wish to serve and honour them, like the Galatians whom Paul sets before us as an example. If it had been possible they would have gladly plucked out their eyes [235] and given them to him. For although the task and the gift belong not to the ministers but to the Lord, because in this word and gift we receive eternal life, and everything that we could ever wish or desire, our admiration of this gift leads to those who bring us such a gift also being precious and dear to us. All help and gifts come entirely from God; yet how highly even the world honours those through whom it receives an abundance of good things, whether they be health, riches, honours, dignities, or whatever else is precious and highly valued in the eyes of the world.

May our dear God grant that we should all well consider this example of the Galatians brought before us by the fifth *[fourth]* text, noticing that these were blessed, as the apostle testifies concerning them, when they were affectionately disposed towards their carer of souls, Paul; but when their hearts grew cold towards Paul, [112(f4)a] they were led astray, captive and wretched, and gave themselves over to the erroneous and pernicious enchantment of the false apostles instead of the blessed obedience of Paul.

How the most powerful emperors submitted themselves to the church's ministry.

All God-fearing people have always been faithful in observing this obedience, however high and great in worldly authority they may have been. When the bishops wanted to accuse and blame one another in an unseemly way about stupid and trifling matters before him Constantine, that so glorious and powerful emperor, took their letters of complaint and burned them up, exhorting them to

peace and unity and saying to them: 'God has given you authority to judge over us, and we should be judged by you, not you by
us.' And when the election of the Bishop of Milan was to take
place, in which St Ambrose was chosen, Emperor Valentinian I
told the bishops whom he had summoned to the election: 'Elect
one to whom we, who rule the empire, may submit our heads with
a good conscience, and whose punishment we, when because we
are human we sin, may receive as the treatment of a physician.' We
have described in the ninth chapter above how the great and godly
emperor Theodosius submitted himself in penance to St Ambrose.
[236] Thus all true believers have always submitted and yielded themselves to the Lord's ministers and word.

The papists have reversed the meaning of what Constantine said.

However, the papists have drawn a false conclusion from all this,
maintaining that all authority should be subordinate to the spiritual
sword [112(f4)b] that they wield, and they should be subject to no-
one; that they should judge everyone and yet not be judged by
anyone, however ungodly and shameful their teaching and lives
might be. This does not mean that we should discount these blessed words and examples of pious emperors, but we should regard
them as Christian words set before us as Christian examples, and
tell the papists that in a false and ungodly way they have reversed
the meaning of the words and examples of these pious princes.
For it was certainly not the intention of dear Constantine or these
other godly princes that they should not judge ungodly bishops, or
that just because they were called bishops everyone should submit
himself to their ungodly malice; because these emperors always
deposed wicked bishops whose teaching or lives were ungodly
from their sees, consigning them to misery and punishing them by
imprisonment or execution. This is shown by the histories and laws
of these emperors, which we still have.

The pious Constantine, Valentinian and other godly emperors understood their statements about the power and authority of bishops in this way: the bishops should live blameless lives and remedy their own faults, so that no-one needed to punish or judge them, because it was their responsibility to dispense God's word and by it to judge all believers and lead them to reformation of life; and that therefore the temporal sword and all authority should be subject to the spiritual sword and authority. But [113(g1)a] this spiritual sword is the word of God, not the malice of the false so-called bishops. And if the carers of souls administer and wield this spiritual sword, the word of God, properly, since all things are created through God's word, then all people should submit themselves with the highest and most perfect degree of subjection and obedience to them, or rather to the word of the Lord which they teach and according to which they judge; and let not the human ministers themselves, but Christ, the heavenly King, in and through his ministers, judge and govern them by his word.

This is why we should faithfully pray that the Lord would grant us [237] to note all these things well; that in his ministers it is himself, our only Saviour, whom we hear; and that if we obey them we are obeying and following him to eternal life; and that if we do not obey and follow them, but despise them, it is himself whom we are not hearing and are despising to our own eternal perdition.

Significance of the seventh and eighth texts.

Thus if the faithful ministers are acting in his name with us and for our eternal salvation, if they are labouring and bearing troubles for us, if they are ministering to us for our eternal life, then we should love them all the more for the sake of this blessed and beneficial work, as we are admonished in the seventh text; and should we perhaps think that they are dealing with us too roughly and handling us too severely, we should still be at peace with them, having regard to the Lord, the beneficial work they do and the fact that they are guarding over our souls, and obey them, not distressing them by our disobedience and thus making their ministry [113(g1)b] and work bitter to them. For to do this can only do the greatest harm to us, as the eighth text admonishes and shows us.

What is required is obedience to Christ, not to the ministers.

But this obedience, this respect, high estimation, love and honour for ministers are all to be offered in the Lord, and to the extent that they are serving the Lord, not men or themselves. We do not want at this point to re-open a door to any form of tyranny or carnal arrogance. We have already explained what sort of elders and ministers of the care of souls churches are to have: faithful ministers of Christ who are seeking, doing and managing things in the church not in any way for themselves or for any other person or creature, but only for Christ. These are the ones whom Christ's sheep should obey with all their hearts as the ministers of Christ, giving them the greatest respect and showing them all love and service in the Lord.

They are not to be thoughtless and suspect evil of them; they are not to turn upside down their teaching and work in the Lord, or accept all kinds of lies and disparagement of them straight away and without evidence. This is something, sadly, that Satan is always arousing and bringing about in many people, in order that the work of our salvation may be pitifully damaged and foiled to the appalling disadvantage of many, by the introduction of pernicious sects and heresies and by apostasy into all manner of carnal and mad living. We were most anxious to guard pious consciences against this deceit and attack of Satan, through which all the fruit of the holy gospel would be wretchedly destroyed, showing them that they should not by any means become the slaves of men.

[238] [114(g2)a] Let everyone take note that this is what he must above all and always hear from Christ's ministers: Repent, for the kingdom of God is near. But where there should be repentance, instead there will be failings and errors. This is why everyone needs to be disposed to the glad acceptance of correction and teaching, and to judge and think of those who are over him as he does of everyone, according to genuine love; being confident of them that they have his good at heart and are seeking his salvation. Let everyone pray to the Lord that he might grant us to hear his voice, not that of a stranger. Let everyone then hear and consider what he says with true singleness of heart, seeking Christ the Lord alone and thinking about what is said to him in Christ's name. Then the Lord will certainly guard him against all false doctrine, and above all from giving too much attention to human authority, and will enable him to recognize and keep his word so that he might amend his life and attain eternal salvation, even if all those who are heard in the ministry of the care of souls may err or be unfaithful. In this way every Christian will protect himself against any pernicious disobedience and contempt of Christ in his ministers, and also guard and keep himself from all false human tyranny, under Christ's yoke and in his kingdom.

That concludes what we wanted to remind and exhort readers at the end of this little book concerning the obedience of Christ's sheep. This is certainly something which, in the case of many at this time, is no less essential to learn and consider than the previous points we covered. May the Lord grant them singleness of heart, and that they may truly love his kingdom, not the liberty of the flesh. Then they will faithfully help to promote all the [114(g2)b] articles in this book, not only in themselves but in others, above all in their prayers to the Lord, and also with all Christian diligence and persistence, as much as the calling of each one allows him to promote them.

A Summary of This Little Book

Firstly, that we are all to be properly united in Christ, being his true body and thus members of one another in him, and to show to our fellows in the faith and to everyone the true fellowship of his word, the holy sacraments, Christian discipline, and also all counsel and help in things both corporal and spiritual: this is taught by the first chapter of this little book.

In this way the kingdom of Christ will truly be with us, and he the Lord will himself [239] lead and rule us to eternal life until the end of the world; this is what the second chapter instructs us.

And the Lord will give us his true and faithful ministers, and through them will work mightily among us, so that we may be born again and be built up day by day, in order that his kingdom might constantly grow and become stronger among us. The third chapter tells us about this.

And in order that he might carry out the work of our salvation through these ministers of his as smoothly as possible, he will appoint and ordain them to this work of our salvation in the most orderly way according to the particular needs and variations of this ministry, so that the congregation is provided through them with all spiritual and bodily counsel, and no-one suffers from [115(g3)a] bodily or spiritual deprivation. And in order that this two-fold ministry, to the spiritual and to the physical, may be carried out as effectively as possible, he will also grant that these ministers should themselves see that there is fitting order among themselves, and arrange things so that nothing is omitted in any way, but everything is carried out in the best way for the church and the house of God. This is set forth in the fourth chapter.

Then we will also faithfully serve the Lord by means of the orderly election and ordination of all ranks and varieties of ministers of the church, so that we might receive and have those who are trusted and loved by all, and also skilled and keen in carrying out this ministry and the true care of souls. This is what the fifth chapter tells us.

In this way the five tasks of the care of souls will be rightly practised: those of searching for and finding all the lost sheep, bringing back the strays, healing the injured, strengthening the ailing, and guarding the healthy ones and feeding them in the right way. These differences in Christ's sheep and the ministry of the care of souls towards them are explained in the sixth chapter.

Then all the churches of Christ, but principally among them rulers, and most directly and actually carers of souls, are to employ all diligence and labour in order that the lost sheep, i.e. Christ's elect who do not yet acknowledge him and are not yet in his sheep-pen, may be gathered among his sheep and come into his communion, and live in the complete obedience of the gospel. This is taught by the seventh chapter.

These also, each according to his calling, [115(g3)b] will be concerned and assist in the restoring to the true and full communion of Christ of the stray sheep, i.e. all those who have been led away from the church to carnal excess or spiritual sects and heresies, as the eighth chapter describes.

And also they will see that the injured sheep, i.e. all those who, although they remain in God's church, fall into more serious sins, breaking and injuring [240] their spiritual limbs in the life of Christ, may be bandaged and healed by means of timely recollection of their sins, and salutary discipline and penance, with the imposition of mortification of the flesh, that is, that they might be enabled to attain true believing repentance and notable reformation of life. This is taught by the ninth chapter. Also in this chapter the true practice of discipline and penance in the church, as it was ordained by the Lord and maintained for the good of the church by the apostles and ancient holy fathers, and should be instituted and used again by us for the sake of true reformation, was somewhat extensively explained and proved, and all sorts of objections which are raised by some against this practice of discipline and penance were refuted.

Similarly they are to see that the ailing and weak sheep, i.e. all those who remain in the church and do not fall into more serious sins, but are stupid and immature in faith, love, discipline and patience, that is, in the whole of Christian life, may be strengthened in true Christian life and made more and more enthusiastic and earnest in seeking all that is good. This we have spoken about in the tenth chapter.

Then they are also to see that the healthy sheep, i.e. those who remain in the church of God and conduct themselves within it in a good and [116(g4)a] Christian way, do not fall into serious sins or in some other way become dull and slack in the Christian life, are protected against all trouble and fed in a truly Christian way so that all that is good may be encouraged; and that they do not lack anything in Christian teaching and admonition, either in the congregation or individually; and also that for the good of the sheep those who might corrupt and trouble them by their disorderly lives and examples should be excluded from the fellowship of the sheep. This is set out in the eleventh chapter.

In the twelfth and final chapter we have also described the true obedience owed by Christ's sheep to the care of souls and those responsible for it, and how necessary and how perfect this obedience must be; and also how we can ensure that someone does not take upon himself a strange yoke under the guise and in place of the yoke of Christ, but remains and shows himself to be completely committed and obedient to the carers of souls, as to the Lord himself.

That is the content and summary of this little book, which we have written solely for the Lord's glory and for the improvement of his church at this time when Christ's sheep are so deplorably scattered, commending it to the Christian consideration of all God's children, asking only that nothing should be judged according to carnal standards, but everything according to the word of the Lord. May the Lord grant that it will be of much use for his kingdom. For indeed, this [241] work of the true care of souls, ordained by the Lord and so necessary for the welfare of the church, is still properly understood by very few. May the Lord make it properly understood and dear to us all. Amen.

By

M. BUCER,

AT THE BEHEST OF HIS FELLOW-WORKERS
IN THE WORD OF THE LORD IN
THE CHURCH AT STRASBOURG.

APPENDIX I

CONCERNING THE 'MARRIED PRIESTS'
(A NOTE BY ROBERT STUPPERICH)

For his understanding of the Pauline expression 'husband of one wife' Bucer refers to John Chrysostom's exegesis of the relevant passages. In his dispute with Bartholomæus Latomus in *Scripta duo adversaria D. Bartholomaei Latomi LL. Doctoris, et Martini Buceri theologi* of 1544 he expounds in detail his understanding of Chrysostom's passages in the section on celibacy (pp. 76ff.). In the first place he deals with the exposition of 1 Timothy 3. On this Chrysostom remarks that Paul uses the words *'unius uxoris vir'* because the Jews had been allowed *'secundas adire nuptias et duas semel habere uxores'*. But by this, according to Bucer's understanding, Chrysostom is not referring to two separate things—i.e., to use the language of the later church law, *bigamia successiva* and *bigamia vera*—but is emphasizing the same thing by using a double expression: it is only *bigamia vera* which is forbidden. Bucer goes on to consider the exposition by Chrysostom of Titus 1: in Titus 1 Paul is attacking heretics who completely condemn marriage, and at the same time he focusses his attention against certain *impudici,* whom he does not wish to be admitted to church office following a second marriage *(post secundas nuptias): 'nam qui erga defunctam uxorem nullam servavit benevolentiam, quomodo bonus ecclesiæ præsul esse potuerit?'* From this Bucer concludes that Chrysostom is only attacking second marriages *'lascivorum et impudicorum hominum'* and those *'qui viva uxore sua legitima alteram duxerit'*, or *'qui duas habuerit simul'*, or *'qui alteram repudiata priore habuerit'*. In any case the Latin translation is wrong. The word ἀπελθοῦσαν cannot be rendered into Latin as *'defunctam'*, but should be translated with a part of the verb *'abire'*. From this it seems obvious to Bucer that the ecclesiastical exegesis according to which the passage of Paul means that a priest may only have one wife in his whole life is a peculiar opinion of the oriental fathers Ambrose, Jerome and Augustine. But a private opinion like this may not be made into a rule for the church. Chrysostom's exegesis is more suitable to Paul, and may not be pushed aside. Even Jerome quotes the exegesis of the Greek fathers without dismissing it.

It is very doubtful if Bucer's understanding of the passages in Chrysostom is accurate. The *Thesaurus Græcæ Linguæ* under ἀπέρξεσθαι gives an abundance of references with the meaning *'mori'*. It is to be noted in addition that the meaning *'mori'* is common in biblical writing and in the fathers. Also current practice forbids the priests of the orthodox churches to marry a second time after the death of their first wife.

The question of a second marriage had become a topical one in Strasbourg through the case of Capito, who in the year 1531 after the death of his first wife married Wibrandis Rosenblatt, Œcolampadius' widow. This marriage led to the question of irregularity *ex defectu sacramentis*.

APPENDIX 2

CONCERNING CHURCH GUARDIANS

St Thomas' Archives, Strasbourg, No. 38
[Church Guardians ... Bucer 1532]
Original in the Hand of Konrad Hubert

It is fitting for the true Christian always to move forwards and not backwards, to increase and not decrease in all that is good; and since the enemy always sows his bad seed among God's good wheat, and where he can creates contempt of God's word, division and schism, our gracious lords in an honourable counsel for the maintenance of Christian unity and promotion of true Christian life have appointed to each benefice or parish three church guardians: one from the standing council, the second from the jurors, and the third from the congregation. Those who have been appointed in our parish are N., N. and N.

Among other things this office involves having a special oversight over the pastors and deacons, and if they hear, see or learn from others that there is something blameworthy in their life, teaching or preaching, they are to admonish them or correct them in a friendly way. And in everything which according to what is found in scripture is required for the office of the care of souls and proper feeding of Christ's lambs, these guardians are to join faithfully with all the pastors and deacons, so that they might to the best of their ability be advised and assisted in order that the building up of the local churches might be promoted through all their preaching and other church activities, as set out in the rules which they have been given. And if anyone desires the preachers and their assistants to give account of their faith, doctrine or life, this is to take place before these church guardians, either together or individually, as opportunity at the time shall determine. On this matter we now admonish you in the Lord, that if anyone has any complaint or accusation of shortcoming against us or ours, touching doctrine or life, and he has not managed to sort it out with us, he should refer it to the appointed church guardians, so that the matter may be faithfully dealt with and put right, as in many cases has happened. If not, he should still be given a good Christian explanation with which he may be content. Our whole salvation consists in our being and continuing to be of one mind in the true faith, and this cannot be the case unless a person is of one mind in Christian doctrine and remains so in his estimation of it. [245] That is why the enemy of the truth is always seeking to divide the children of God in their doctrine, and make them despise doctrine, always using this so that by means of lies he can belittle and ruin those responsible for doctrine. For he knows well that doctrine cannot bring forth fruit in those by whom the ministers of the word are despised and hated. Therefore, dear friends, let us beware of the enemy and always strive for Christian unity. And if anyone has a complaint against us, let him make use of the means we have now suggested, and in that way, God willing, he will be quite satisfied. And let us ask God to grant these church guardians and ourselves, together with the whole congregation, to seek earnestly the kingdom of heaven, and constantly and most faithfully to undertake and untiringly to practise everything that may serve to the building up of that kingdom. Amen.